THE RESEARCH-INFORMED TEACHING REVOLUTION

A HANDBOOK FOR THE 21ST CENTURY TEACHER

CHRIS BROWN

JANE FLOOD

GRAHAM HANDSCOMB

First published 2020

by John Catt Educational Ltd,
15 Riduna Park, Station Road,
Melton, Woodbridge IP12 1QT
Tel: +44 (0) 1394 389850
Fax: +44 (0) 1394 386893
Email: enquiries@johncatt.com
Website: www.johncatt.com

ISBN: 978 912906 83 3

Set and designed by John Catt Educational Limited

CONTENTS

ACKNOWLEDGEMENTS

This book would not have been possible without the power of the world wide web and personal commitment to sharing knowledge and expertise; at no point in the writing of this book have the three of us been in the same room, but this has proved to be no obstacle! In the words of Aristotle, when working together and with the contributors, 'The whole is greater than the sum of its parts.' We would also like to thank the contributors for their assiduous efforts in helping create what we believe is not only a readable and extremely engaging book, but also an incredibly useful one. We are indebted to all of you and consider ourselves very lucky to have been able to work with you.

ABOUT THE EDITORS

Chris Brown: Professor Chris Brown is Professor in Education at Durham University's School of Education. Chris has a longstanding interest in how evidence can aid education policy and practice, and this is his 7th book in this area (and his 12th overall). He has also presented and keynoted on the subject at a number of international conferences stretching the globe, from Africa to South America, and has extensive experience of leading a range of funded projects, many of which seek to help teachers identify and scale up best practice. In 2018 Chris was awarded a Stiftung Mercator Foundation Senior Fellowship. Each year, Stiftung Mercator identifies and invites just six people worldwide to apply for one of its fellowships. Potential Fellows are identified by a panel as 'exceptionally talented and outstanding researchers and practitioners' from areas seen as relevant to the themes and fields of activity of Stiftung Mercator. The purpose of the Mercator Fellowship programme is to offer selected fellows the space and freedom to also devote themselves to exploratory and unconventional research and practical projects (typically for six months). Previous Fellows include advisors to former US president Barack Obama and current French president Emmanuel Macron.

Jane Flood: Jane has been an infant teacher for more than 20 years, working in a variety of schools in various roles; from supply teacher to head, in one-form entry infants to large inner-city primaries. Achieving an MA(Ed) in 1998, completing a Best Practice Research Scholarship 2001–2002, a Recognition in Excellence in Inquiry Based learning in Science Education (IBSE) Certificate in 2014, and in 2018 becoming a Founding Fellow of the Chartered College of Teaching, throughout her career Jane has engaged in school-based research designed to raise pupil outcomes and involving the dissemination of this learning to colleagues. Jane is studying part time for a PhD at Durham University, focusing on ways to manage the competing priorities of teacher researchers and informal leaders in research learning networks. She has presented this work at national and international conferences. She is currently head at Netley Marsh C of E Infant School.

Graham Handscomb: Graham is Visiting Professor at University College London (UCL) and was Professor of Education and Dean of The College of Teachers. He has had an extensive career of senior leadership of local authorities and schools and 20 years' teaching experience. He was external examiner for the University of Wales. He created the online Master's in Educational Practice leadership programmes for the Welsh Government and the online leadership and management master's programme for the University of Nottingham. Graham has made a considerable contribution to the development of school-based practitioner enquiry and pioneered the concept of the 'research-engaged school'. He wrote the criteria to establish the national Research Mark award for the National Foundation for Educational Research. As an educational consultant, he works with schools, teaching school alliances and trusts throughout the UK and also has a range of international experience. He was a senior member of Hughes Hall, University of Cambridge, and is a fellow of numerous universities. Over many years, Graham has exercised a major influence on professional development policy and practice. He is editor of *Professional Development Today* and on the editorial boards of a number of other academic publications, including *Creative Teaching and Learning*.

FOREWORD

LESLEY SAUNDERS

Lesley Saunders is Visiting Professor at UCL Institute of Education and at Newman University, Birmingham; she is an honorary research fellow at the Oxford University Department of Education. Lesley is also an award-winning and published poet.

Some revolutions are abrupt and sometimes also short-lived. Others take the form of a long-term choreography: two steps forward, two to the side and even a step or two backwards – as a *reculer pour mieux sauter*, perhaps. So it has been with research-informed teaching, which over the decades has been variously scored – as it were – for full-blown romantic ballets of 'teacher-led curriculum development' as well as for the hard-edged contemporary theatre of 'evidence-based practice'. This book gives us a powerful sense of how all that dedication, skill, insight and collaborative learning has enriched our experience of education, in whatever roles we find ourselves; and also a sense of what kinds of innovations in concept, approach and design we might hope to see in future.

The way in which the relationship between teaching and research is conceptualised reveals, amongst other things, the assumptions being made about the profession of teaching. So the present developments could be described in terms of a direct continuation of the rhetorical turn towards 'evidence-based education' promoted by New Labour when it came to power in 1997: the espousal of evidence was intended to signal the end of ideology as the key determinant of decision-making.

This was a disingenuous gesture, of course, since ideologies of one kind or another, as well as values and principles, have continued to exert a justifiable influence on decision-making at every level of the system. Even so, the basic idea sounded persuasive enough to both decision-makers and researchers that, in effect, they colluded with each other to permit some assumptions to flourish: for example, that decisions should be based on evidence above all else; that it is the principal job of researchers to produce that evidence; and even that the methods that will give results that can count as evidence can and should be tightly prescribed. Teachers need to use such results to improve their practice or run the risk of being thought unprofessional. Research thus becomes part of the apparatus of accountability, under the guise of valorising 'what works'.

On the other hand, the idea that teaching should be a research-informed profession is more accurately located back in the 1980s, with the foundational work of Lawrence Stenhouse, who taught us to think of research and teaching as dialectically connected in and through the day-to-day reflexive expertise of teacher-scholars. This is why many educators have come to believe that the idea of 'research-informed' practice is different from, subtler and ultimately more demanding than that of 'evidence-based' practice.

Part of the difficulty with 'evidence-based' practice lies in its apparent definitiveness, its implied certainty. 'Research-informed' practice, by contrast, helps us to think of research as a form of specialised knowledge which is created, not as a product made elsewhere and then disseminated to and applied by the 'users' of research, but through a process which is collaborative, reflexive and discursive, is wholly comfortable with provisionality, and can make room for the contribution of different kinds of expertise – including the expert knowledge that experienced teachers have integrated into their repertoire and which enables them to respond and improvise, light-footedly and in the moment, in each and every different classroom situation.

'Pedagogy' is consequently the word I find myself reaching for, and Robin Alexander's definition of pedagogy continues to be worth quoting:

'the act of teaching together with its attendant theory and discourse, which are collective, generalisable and open to public scrutiny. It is what one needs to know, and the skills one needs to command, in order to make and justify the many different kinds of decision of which teaching is constituted' (Alexander 2004, p. 11).

The practices of both teaching and research are subtle and many-faceted, are cognitively, ethically and emotionally demanding, and are deeply dependent on specialised learning and expertise. They are art as well as science. Integrating the processes of, and insights from, research into the daily routines of the classroom (and vice versa) is therefore intrinsically challenging. The range of issues which the contributors to this book address and the contrasting perspectives they represent not only are interesting and worthwhile in themselves but also serve to uncover the inescapable complexity – managerial as well as intellectual, social as well as systemic – of the undertaking.

Bringing together the main kinds of institution involved, schools and universities, continues to be a large part of the challenge – yet this is much more a consequence of the way the education system operates in the UK than of any intrinsic differences between the worlds of teaching and research. Still less useful to our future thinking is what Viv Baumfield in her chapter calls 'the binary opposition of theory and practice'. This book invites us to look beyond and behind such casual and unhelpful presumptions and to distil the more durable concepts and possibilities. For example:

- the need to improve the accessibility, readability and actionability of high-quality research (that is, peer-reviewed and underpinned by explicit and attested theories, and synthesised wherever possible); this is not a question of preferring particular methods but of ensuring fit-for-purpose methodologies;
- the need to identify more clearly the advantages, and the disadvantages, of using social media to communicate research;
- the need to support teachers and school leaders to exercise critical judgement in considering whether particular approaches developed

elsewhere are relevant to their context; and to make a realistic assessment of how much improvement can be genuinely accomplished;

- the necessity of espousing a theory of change – that is, an understanding of how changes in practice come about and how they can be sustained;
- the need to have elaborated conceptualisations of professional practice, professional knowledge and professional learning in which collaborative inquiry and research engagement are central;
- the value and importance of communities of inquiry, not least in the form of sustainable partnerships between academic and teacher researchers;
- the need to develop a common educational discourse of scholarship which is shared by academic researchers and teachers;
- the potential of the 'research champion' or 'knowledge broker' role – who could be an individual or a small team – in changing the school culture as well as supporting specific projects;
- the need for policy-makers to acknowledge and address the systemic obstacles (such as the perverse incentives in current accountability frameworks and procedures).

That is the conspicuous value this book adds to the enterprise, by marshalling so many different points of view into a panoptic vision of what might be as well as of what is.

My own recent small-scale experience as an assessor for Research Mark accreditation awarded by the National Foundation for Educational Research[1] to research-active schools indicates that schools would do well to:

- strengthen the links between inquiry projects and school development planning and priority-setting;
- share inquiry processes and outcomes more thoroughly (for example, through peer mentoring, cross-phase/-subject projects and by embedding research engagement into CPD culture);

1.   NFER Research Mark: www.bit.ly/2Guc3kI

- allocate appropriate and sufficient resource of time and personnel;
- strengthen critical questioning and interpretation as part of research methodology;
- enrich the role of pupils and students in internal research projects;
- foster research leadership;
- involve governors;
- extend research engagement to other staff, such as teaching assistants.

That many of both these sets of ideas and suggestions have been previously aired (as several of the contributors emphasise) is testament not only to their enduring importance, but also to the evident and pressing need for a national system that better enables consistency, continuity and sustainability of such foundational initiatives and processes. To return to the fanciful metaphor with which I began, we might one day dream about bringing together research and teaching in the form of a dance to the music of time, with all the collective refinement, grace and verve of a supremely accomplished corps de ballet.

REFERENCES
Alexander, R. (2004) 'Still no pedagogy? Principle, pragmatism and compliance in primary education', *Cambridge Journal of Education* 34 (1) pp. 7–33.

INTRODUCTION

CHRIS BROWN, JANE FLOOD AND GRAHAM HANDSCOMB

We know a lot about teachers and research. We know that they should mix and there can be significant benefits if they do so, but we also know that teachers and research often fail to socialise. We think of it like hosting a house party where one group of friends won't leave the kitchen while another colonises the lounge. But in our view the party would be so much better if all your friends circulated or, perhaps better still, congregated in some common ground (although preferably not the bathroom). To try to remedy this situation we decided to bring together the best in the business – leading thinkers and doers working in this area – and asked them to tell us what they have learned about connecting research and practice and to give their general take on the subject. The results, as we hope you will agree, are illuminating, and provide a wealth of advice and perspectives on the subject.

Of the practitioners contributing, we have those working across schools for teaching school alliances. For instance, **Sarah Seleznyov**, who discusses the power of using one or two teachers to achieve change, the need to build the research capacity of staff, and the reasons that teachers are required to have a deep understanding of why it is believed an evidence-informed change will actually make a difference. Likewise is **Hanna Miller**, who, like Sarah, has used a 'change agent' type approach (the Cognition Crew) to try to scale up good practice. We have teachers providing their perspectives from engaging with research at the classroom level. **Adam Boxer**, for example, discusses the much-acknowledged issue of how to lead change effectively. We also have school leaders – including **Lindsay Palmer** and Dr **Marcella McCarthy** – who provide practical case studies of how to embed research-informed cultures and effective approaches to connecting research and practice and detail how research use has transformed their schools. Overcoming some of the practical barriers to research use are nicely discussed here by **Claire Harley**.

Our academic contributors include **Dom Wyse**, President of the British Educational Research Association and Professor of Early Childhood and Primary Education, who explores how teachers or school leaders can decide which research to pay attention to. A similar theme is examined by **Raphael Wilkins** as well as Professor **Steve Higgins**, who authored the Education Endowment Foundation's *Teaching and Learning Toolkit*, and uses his chapter to examine the potential contribution it can make (and has made) to research-informed teaching. Professor **Vivienne Baumfield** augments Steve's chapter by taking a 'close to practice' approach to consider different forms of knowledge and the consequences of these for how we think about practice and research. Professor **Stephen Gorard** meanwhile looks at what research says about the best approaches to get research into schools; while Professor **Graham Handscomb**, who pioneered the concept, discusses what it means to be a research-engaged school, and how to achieve the type of engagement that makes research use meaningful.

We have input from other key players including edu-blogger Dr **Gary Jones**, who discusses how to promote and share research effectively through the use of social media, and **Cat Scutt**, Director of Education and Research at the Chartered College of Teaching, the professional body for the teaching profession. In her chapter, Cat links research use to teacher professionalisation and outlines the need to (and how to) tackle the individual, school and systemic factors holding research use back. Similar themes are explored by **Andrew Morris**, chair of the Coalition for Evidence-Based Education; **Jonathan Haslam**, Director at the Institute for Effective Education; and **Karen Wespieser**, social researcher and founder of #UKEdResChat, who makes a strong case for a more effective link between researchers and schools. We are also fortunate to have **Maria Cunningham** and **David Weston** from the Teacher Development Trust, who outline the need to consider people and culture as much as processes and resources, again tapping into some of the key factors that affect the success (or not) of change initiatives. And a fantastic contribution from Dr **Julie Nelson**, Senior Research Manager at the National Foundation for Educational Research, sets out how schools can use 'identify, use and review' cycles to help them embed research in practice. Julie also outlines other freely available resources that can help schools establish where they are and move forward with their research-informed journey.

We finish with a chapter of our own that corrals all of the ideas presented and which we hope provides good practical guidance on how you can link research and teaching within and across schools (our guide to the ultimate party!). After curating all of the chapters, we feel they are packed with insight and that, in putting the book together, we have produced something truly comprehensive. But we are not people to rest on our laurels, so if you think a key idea or case study is still out there, we'd love to hear from you!

Chris, Jane and Graham.
@ChrisBrown1475, @JaneFlood14, graham@handscomb-consultancy.co.uk

REALLY CHANGING PRACTICE
HELPING TEACHERS TO EMBED LEARNING FROM RESEARCH

SARAH SELEZNYOV (*@sarahseleznyov*)

Sarah Seleznyov is Director of London South Teaching School Alliance, home to Charles Dickens Research School. Sarah has been a deputy head and a school improvement consultant and variously held roles at UCL Institute of Education, the Fischer Family Trust and the National Literacy Trust. Sarah's research specialism is teacher professional development, and she has published widely on Japanese lesson study.

GETTING EVIDENCE INTO THE HANDS OF TEACHERS

As Director of a research school and teaching school alliance, with a heavy focus on developing evidence-informed practice, there have been two key challenges for us: firstly, getting teachers to read and discuss the research; secondly and most significantly, making sure that the education evidence with which teachers engage becomes embedded in classroom practice, and ideally beyond the person who directly engages with the research. The real trick is to get evidence into the hands of a small number of teachers and to enable them to change the practice of the school, meaning a positive impact on learning for all pupils.

This chapter details some of the strategies we have used which do enable real changes to classroom practice that align with the best evidence we have about teaching and learning.

REALLY READING THE RESEARCH

Teachers are busy people and generally not confident academics. They cannot easily access educational research and do not have time to read series of journal articles to develop a deep understanding of an issue; nor do they usually have the skills to read articles critically. However, only reading overviews and blogs doesn't really provide an in-depth understanding of a research field. Here are some techniques we have used to overcome these challenges.

1. TEACH THE SKILLS OF CRITICALLY READING RESEARCH

We never expect teachers to read an article before a professional development session, because we know teachers are busy people. We run regular 'Exploring The Evidence' sessions for teachers across the alliance, in which we explore recent research and help teachers to engage with it critically, making their own judgements as to its relevance for them.

In every session, we work through a key sequence of thinking:

Why has this been written?

The facilitator introduces the paper under discussion, explaining where the paper comes from and why it was published.

Why are we reading it?

The facilitator explains why this paper may be interesting and/or relevant.

What are the authors saying that is relevant to what I want to find out?

Teachers work in small groups to read a key section of the text, interrogating its meaning and relevance to them as practitioners. They then share their section with all, ensuring everyone has an overview of the full text.

How convincing is what the authors are saying?

The facilitator encourages teachers to consider possible limitations of the research. Is it statistically valid? Is it relevant to their context? Might the author be biased? Does it conflict with other known evidence?

What can I make out of this?
Teachers discuss how they might apply the findings in their own classrooms.

This sequence of thinking supports critical engagement with research beyond the session: once teachers have been through the process collaboratively, they can internalise it, enabling them to read critically across a range of education evidence.

2. BREAK THE RESEARCH DOWN INTO CHUNKS

Drawn from Stoll and Brown's work on research engagement (2015), this technique has successfully enabled teachers to engage with a large body of research and reflect on which parts of it have relevance or meaning for them. This technique relies on the production of a literature review, written in plain English, which covers around 20–30 studies on a broad theme. Around 20–30 significant chunks of text (sentences or short paragraphs) from the literature review are printed onto strips of paper, and teachers are asked to discuss them collaboratively, clustering them into themes. They then label and map the clusters, comparing their classifications with other groups. This process makes sure teachers really read the literature review: you cannot map and cluster the strips unless you have all read and thought about their meaning.

Teachers are then asked which of the strips resonate with them in their context. This helps them develop their own lines of enquiry. When they are then provided with the full literature review, they can find their strip and read it in its context, going on to access it in its original source: the underlying journal article. In this way, teachers engage fully with quite challenging and lengthy academic material: they themselves have identified its value and are following their own lines of enquiry.

REALLY USING EVIDENCE TO CHANGE PRACTICE

Of course, as any school leader knows, really reading the evidence is only the first step. What really matters is taking that evidence into classroom practice so that it can make a difference to pupil learning.

As a general rule, we have found that one of the best ways to make this happen is to engage teachers in cycles of iterative enquiry in their own classroom: put simply, teacher professional development that takes a research approach really changes practice. At its simplest, Hargreaves calls this 'tinkering' (1999), a process of 'haphazard trial and error' in the classroom. Timperley, Kaser and Halbert's model is of 'spirals of inquiry' (2014) involving repeated cycles of identifying problems, really understanding them, taking action, and checking impact. Research lesson study (Seleznyov, 2018) uses live classroom practice to engage teachers in similar cycles of research and reflection.

All our professional development approaches try to adopt this structure, helping teachers work collaboratively to really understand and use evidence to change practice. The stages we build into all professional development programmes are:

1. Engage with the evidence.
2. Have a focus group in mind.
3. Generate a research question.
4. Baseline current practice.
5. Based on this data and the evidence, design a change to practice.
6. Implement the change with expert support, adapting it as it embeds.
7. Engage the wider school in your project.
8. Gather impact data.
9. Assess success and share with colleagues.
10. Plan for next steps.

We have found that stages 2 and 4 are crucial to gain buy-in from teachers. If teachers are able to select a group of focus pupils, this makes their use of the evidence more meaningful to them. When they are asked to gather baseline and impact data, we support them to design their own tools. We teach them about the relative merits and disadvantages of questionnaires and interviews. They are shown how to design questionnaires in ways that will provide meaningful data: making sure a question is easy to understand; using scaled scores wherever possible; minimising text entries. We also explain to them how to carry out interviews that will get at the information they want: considering who is best placed to get honest answers from interviewees; not over-scaffolding questions; using silence to develop deeper responses. If relevant, we show them ways to code classroom transcripts so that they provide meaningful measurable data.

Using a very unusual technique (Brown, 2017), we also help them to make sense of the data they have gathered. We ask teachers to build a physical model of the situation they are seeking to change, premised on the notion that created props can help teachers make sense of a set of complex data (Stevens, 2013) – see illustrations below. There are always sceptical participants at the beginning of this activity but once they have built their models and shared them with colleagues, teachers feel they have developed a deeper understanding of the issue they are trying to tackle and what the potential solutions might be. It is felt to be so powerful that they often decide to share the models with a wider group of colleagues.

This model shows the barriers to including pupils with autism in the collaborative culture of the classroom, for example language and communication difficulties as represented by the mouth.

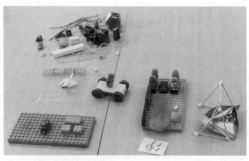

This model shows how the pupil with autism in the class is smoothly supported to access all the different curriculum subject areas.

SCALING UP

Getting teachers to change their practice becomes more problematic when scaling up to key-stage, departmental or whole-school level. Key to tackling this challenge is developing an understanding of what happens in the gap between engaging with the evidence and making the change in the classroom. For us, Hall's (2013) theories of implementation have proved particularly helpful.

Hall (2013) explores implementation of any desired change to practice **along three continuums**. The first helps us understand **whether intent to use will become a reality.** We all know how tricky it is to change a habit. Imagine trying to make sure you floss your teeth more: you know it's good for you; you've seen the evidence; your dentist (the expert) has recommended it. But you are busy, so you have to build up the willpower, make sure you don't get lazy and fall back into old habits, not give up when you've had a few days off, and practise repeatedly until it becomes a new habit. This can be described by Hall and Hord's (2001) levels of use:

1. First you *orient* yourself to the change, getting the information you need to get started.
2. Then you *prepare* to use it and set a start time.
3. Initially, you become a *mechanical user*: you are doing it, but it's awkward and uncomfortable; you need to consciously make an effort to continue to teach in this new way.

4. Soon, use becomes *routine* and the new way of teaching becomes an established habit.
5. You then begin to *refine* the approach, making it work better for you and your pupils.
6. Later you talk to colleagues and work together to *integrate* this new practice across the team so it works successfully for all pupils.
7. Finally, you enter a *renewal* stage, where you begin to make this practice your own as a school.

Understanding where teachers are on this continuum can really help school leaders tailor their support. Hall's (2013) work shows that if teachers never get beyond *mechanical use*, they are very likely to slip back into old habits. He notes that the majority of teachers will be at *mechanical use* for some time. Hall (2013) says these teachers will need practical help to get properly started. Those working at *integration* level will benefit from being given opportunities to collaborate with colleagues.

But implementing an evidence-informed change to practice is not simply about doing it; it's also about **having a deep understanding of the change itself**. Hall (2013) says we need to classify teachers along a second continuum to really understand how to change practice. As Figure 1 shows, when any change to practice is introduced, there will be four types of teachers.

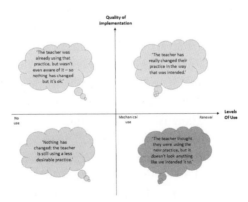

Figure 1: Usage versus quality Adapted from Hall, 2013, p. 281

The first teacher, top left, was already teaching in a way that aligned with the evidence. She hasn't made an effort to change her practice, because she was already (unconsciously) teaching in that way. The second teacher, top right, embraces the change the evidence suggests and starts making a real change to practice, so aligning perfectly with what the evidence suggests. There is no need to worry about either of these teachers.

The teacher at the bottom left, is more of a concern. She exemplifies Hall and Hord's (2001) third continuum: **stages of concern** (2001). Teachers traditionally move from being concerned about their own needs (e.g. wanting information about the change and its implications) to being concerned about the task itself (e.g. workload, time, effort) to finally being concerned about the impact of the change on pupils. It is only at this final stage that the new practice really becomes embedded. This third teacher needs to be helped to understand why the change is important and to believe in the difference it will make to pupils. Enthusiastic colleagues can often help by championing the new practice and demonstrating its impact on learning.

However, our teacher at the bottom right is also a worry. This teacher thinks they are doing exactly what the evidence requires, but when you observe their practice, it bears no relation to the evidence. They haven't understood the intended change, despite having the same input as other teachers. How can we help such teachers to really understand what the new practice should look like? Hall's (2013) advice to help teachers jointly construct an implementation configuration (IC) has proved highly successful in tackling this issue. An IC identifies the key operational components of the new practice in descriptive paragraphs and describes several key variations of each component. The ideal version of the innovation is on the left-hand side (a), with e usually describing traditional or current practices. The process of collaboratively writing the IC helps teachers develop a consensus about what the new practice should look like.

Here is an example of one component from an IC written to help implement peer- and self-assessment:

Pupils use feedback to improve their work				
a	b	c	d	e
There is a balance of time allocated to responding to whole-class and personal feedback. There is strong evidence of pupils using both teacher and peer feedback to improve current and subsequent pieces of work.	There are sometimes lessons taught which provide whole-class feedback and enable pupils to use this to improve past work. Pupils respond to personal feedback from teachers and peers during lessons, rather than on subsequent days, and make improvements to current work. There is some evidence of pupils using teacher and peer feedback to improve subsequent pieces of work.	There is regular time at the start of each lesson allocated to review or respond to feedback. Pupils always read their personal feedback and often act on it to edit and improve past pieces of work; however, there is rarely evidence of this feedback improving subsequent pieces of work.	There is regular lesson time allocated to review or respond to feedback, for example once a week. Pupils sometimes read their personal feedback and there is some evidence of them acting on it to edit and improve past pieces of work.	There is no lesson time allocated to review or respond to feedback. Pupils rarely read their personal feedback and there is no evidence of them acting on it to improve past or subsequent pieces of work.

Using an IC can overcome the problem of teachers reporting (and believing) that they are implementing an evidence-informed change to practice, while its actual presentation is not what you intended.

CONCLUSION: COMPLEXITY, TIME AND PERSISTENCE

In summary, then, the process of getting teachers engaged with research and using it to make real changes to their practice is a complex one. Teachers need to learn how to read research critically and have it presented to them in manageable chunks. Teachers who generate their own evidence through participating in structured collaborative enquiry projects are more likely to use research evidence to change their practice. This is because teacher enquiry projects enable them to own their own problems, help them get a deep understanding of potential solutions and motivate them to develop their own evidence-informed solutions. When scaling up evidence-informed practices, you will encounter both resisters and confused practitioners. Both need personalised support. Hall (2013) offers a practical template for achieving this. And a final note of caution:

major change efforts involve 'complexity, time and persistence and real change takes a minimum of three to five years' (Hall, 2013, p. 265).

TOP TIPS:

- Teach teachers to read research critically, tackling it in manageable chunks.
- Use collaborative teacher enquiry projects to enable deep engagement with evidence.
- Understand why teachers' practice hasn't changed in line with the evidence and tailor your support accordingly.

REFERENCES:

Brown, C. (2017) 'Research learning communities: how the RLC approach enables teachers to use research to improve their practice and the benefits for students that occur as a result', *Research for All* 1 (2) pp. 387–405.

Hall, G. (2013) 'Evaluating change processes: assessing extent of implementation (constructs, methods and implications)', *Journal of Educational Administration* 51 (3) pp. 264–289.

Hall, G. and Hord, S. (2001) *Implementing change: patterns, principles and potholes*. Boston, MA: Allyn and Bacon.

Hargreaves, D. (1999) 'The knowledge-creating school', *British Journal of Educational Studies* 47 (2) pp. 122–144.

Seleznyov, S. (2018) 'Lesson study: an exploration of its translation beyond Japan', *International Journal for Lesson and Learning Studies* 7 (3) pp. 217–229.

Stevens, J. (2013) 'Design as communication in microstrategy: strategic sensemaking and sensegiving mediated through designed artifacts', *AI EDAM* 27 (2) pp. 133–142.

Stoll, L. and Brown, C. (2015) 'Middle leaders as catalysts for evidence-informed change' in Brown, C. (ed.) *Leading the use of research and evidence in schools*. London: Institute of Education Press.

Timperley, H., Kaser, L. and Halbert, J. (2014) *A framework for transforming learning in schools: innovation and the spiral of inquiry*. Melbourne: Centre for Strategic Education.

INTRODUCING
EVIDENCE-INFORMED CHANGE

ADAM BOXER *(@adamboxer1)*

Adam is a Head of Science working in North London. He is a keen promoter of evidence-based practice and has worked in ITT, presented for researchED nationally and internationally, and is the Managing Editor of the CogSciSci learning platform.

UNFULFILLED POTENTIAL

Twenty years ago, education researcher Douglas Carnine expanded on the differences between mature and immature professions (Carnine, 2000). All professions are governed by rules and norms, but whereas immature ones are dominated by folk wisdom, tradition and dogma, mature ones function through evidence, objective data and the search for empirical truth. He argues that professions as diverse as medicine, accounting and seafaring have all, at some point or other, undergone this change. Carnine's 2000 essay argued that the 'pressures to mature are inevitable in education', but it did not assume that they were, at that time, taking place. There were, and still are, many forces working in opposition to such change and Carnine was better placed than most to understand them. Having collaborated extensively with Zig Engelmann, one of the developers of Direct Instruction, Carnine had first-hand experience of working on a programme whose efficacy was rigorously investigated through the largest educational research project ever conducted. Tested against dozens of other teaching methods, Direct Instruction, with its highly structured and scripted explanations, sequenced models, examples and drill, emerged victorious by a significant distance. In comparison with other teaching approaches like enquiry-led learning or constructivist models, it scored highest in terms of not only academic outcomes, but also affective ones: whether or not the students involved **enjoyed** the process.[1]

Engelmann and Carnine were therefore poised at the brink of achieving an educational panacea: a programme that improved students' learning, ability and motivation with the strongest of empirical evidence in its favour. And yet, nothing happened. For a variety of political, social and philosophical reasons, Direct Instruction never quite caught on. One can well understand Carnine's frustration when he wrote that 'in the past – and still today – the profession has tended to respond to such pressures by offering untested but appealing nostrums and innovations that do not improve academic achievement' (2000, p. 10).

SYSTEMATIC OPPOSITION

Decades later, the picture, at least in the UK, has changed considerably. Recent developments such as the rise of researchED and other grassroots organisations have caused an upsurge in teachers engaging with, and indeed demanding, high-quality research evidence. Robust findings from the cognitive sciences are slowly percolating through the education system from the bottom up, and political changes from the top down – like the reformed GCSEs and Ofsted's focus on research – indicate that perhaps that maturation process described by Carnine could be underway.

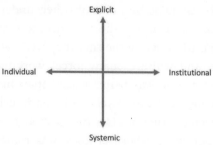

---

1.   For more on Engelmann and Carnine's work, see Boxer, 2019

However, maturation will never be straightforward and there are a host of factors standing in its way. We can classify opposition to this process on a horizontal scale of 'institutional' to 'individual' and a vertical scale of 'explicit' to 'systemic'. For example, when a group of teachers set up an evidence-based teacher training programme, their attempts were described by established figures in initial teacher training as 'arrogant', with aspersions being cast regarding financial motivations (Hazell, 2017).[2] As one of the teachers involved, such explicit opposition was difficult to stomach, and on our axes above it would sit in the top right section. Other organisations might be more willing to change and adapt with the times and with increased focus on evidence-informed practice. However, there is a lack of institutional momentum and change at such levels can be slow and grinding. We could term this 'systemic' opposition: not caused by any particular ideological or theoretical difference of opinion but caused simply by the nature of how institutions organise themselves. Such factors must sit in the bottom right quadrant.

At the other end of our systemic/explicit scale, take a teacher who attends a Saturday conference and listens to a lecture outlining decades of research on the failure of inquiry-based approaches to learning. Returning to their school, they attempt to broach the subject with their teaching and learning lead, only to be told that 'students learn better when they discover things for themselves', with little disagreement being allowed. In this case, it could be that the teachers in the school would be willing to move in a more evidence-informed direction, but progress is halted by the explicit, ideological opposition of one individual, thereby populating the top left quadrant.

In turn, it could be that a curriculum leader is given licence to implement change to move in line with evidence-informed practice. But, on trying to introduce their intervention, they find that it fails to take root simply because teachers do not have the time to adequately adapt, prepare resources, upskill and evaluate on the job. This 'opposition' is endemic in the school systems: it is not a result of

2. The programme was eventually discontinued.

conflicting ideologies, but of factors which are woven into the fabric of our school systems.

The above is not intended simply as an agonising meditation on opposition to evidence-informed practice, but as a tool for establishing a viable route to achieving that aim. In attempting to increase the amount of evidence-informed practice, it is helpful to appreciate that opposition comes in a number of different forms and response must be tailored to the form that is presenting itself. The teacher who wants to convince their deputy head to abandon inquiry-led learning as a whole-school priority must by necessity take a different route to the curriculum leader struggling to manage their team's workload and organisational agility. Without systematic classification and analysis, change will only ever be piecemeal, ad hoc and haphazard.

Over the last three years, I have had the opportunity to work in a team which has increased the evidence-informed nature of its practice in building a new curriculum and adapting pedagogy in its light. Along the journey, there have been opposition forces to be circumnavigated, and below I will give a number of examples and explain how we attempted to deal with them.

TORPOR

Like many other departments in the country, at first we didn't really see the need to change. We came into school, did our jobs with the resources we had available, and went home. We cared deeply, and wanted to do a good job, but broadly we thought things were fine. This was probably a systemic problem, caused not by a lack of desire, but a lack of knowledge-based imagination. We simply did not know at that point that there were better ways to do things. We did not have first-hand experience of seeing departments doing things radically differently. There was no organisational awareness of what 'better' could look like. It was a failure of imagination, but with the acknowledgement that the imaginative lack was domain specific: we couldn't imagine what we, as a better department, would look like.

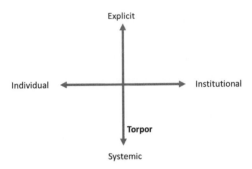

Someone coming into such an environment needs to appreciate the location of this 'opposition'. Going in all guns blazing with radical changes cannot be the right approach, as teachers simply won't understand the **need** for it all. Rather, the approach must be focused in two directions: first, sensitively exposing the shortcomings of the current way of doing things; and second, slowly introducing people to different ideas and visions of success. Exposing team members to practices they won't have encountered before (along with their associated benefits) can slowly remove the torpor and awaken staff's imagination to new possibilities.

This is a long process, and people cannot be expected to suddenly change all their beliefs about education overnight through merely having attended one talk about cognitive load theory or by reading one blog about centralised behaviour systems. It takes time, but simple routes to helping people develop in this area include sending them things to read, inviting colleagues to attend conferences with you, setting up a small reading group (Boxer, 2018) or even just having informal conversations over lunch.

WORKLOAD
Interestingly, there is a secondary effect of the above approach to addressing torpor. Earlier it was mentioned how workload can be a systemic factor preventing individuals from making change. However, this issue is probably better phrased as a 'time resource' opposition, rather than a 'workload' one. People want to do the work; they just do not have the time or resources to do it. On the other hand, if a person does not believe that a particular change is meaningful or helpful, then their

opposition moves to the more 'explicit' end of the axis. Given English education's penchant for introducing meaningless change, such concerns are entirely understandable![3]

Convincing people that the change is meaningful can help counteract this to an extent, but such an endeavour will never be complete without actually reducing the workload. In our project, for example, we showed people how both investing time in high-quality resources and streamlining our bureaucratic processes would, in the long term, reduce their workload.

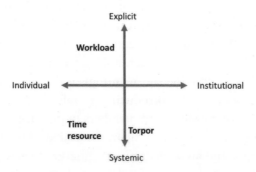

PHILOSOPHICAL CLASH WITH SCHOOL PRIORITIES

There will, inevitably, be some changes that can clash with wider school priorities. Our department slowly moved to lessons centring around explicit, teacher-led instruction, and concurrently featured fewer practical activities, 'engaging' lesson resources and group work. A concern arose that by omitting such practices we were ridding our classrooms of 'joy' – which, at the time, was a school priority. Without a doubt, there was potential for lessons to become dry and unexciting lectures; but this wasn't actually our point of disagreement, which was more about conceptualising terms than pedagogy. Under a conceptualisation of 'joy', our lessons were indeed joyless. If joy in learning is thought to come as a product of engaging and relevant activities, group work and student-led learning, then our lessons were never going to be joyful: they lacked these

3.   See, for example, DfE (2016) *Teacher workload survey 2016*. Retrieved from: www.bit.ly/3aLeM7z [Accessed 17 November 2019].

features. However, it was our belief that real joy was not a surface-level engagement springing from superficial activities but a deep, long-term motivation and drive to succeed springing from a feeling of competence in the subject.[4]

	Conception of joy 1	Conception of joy 2
Expression	In the moment	Over the long term
Springs from	Engaging and relevant activities	Competence and mastery of challenging material

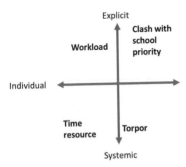

Addressing this is complicated, as fundamentally there is an irreconcilable difference of opinion in how 'joy' is conceptualised, with little choice but to tackle it head on. Start by convincing your team to view things differently, and then start broaching the topic with other power players. It may be helpful to collect student testimonials in response to lesson activities. You should be explicit with your students that with time they will get better at your subject, and that these achievements will be celebrated and will lead to feelings of satisfaction. Then, whenever students express those feelings (prompted or unprompted), make a careful record to inform future discussions. With time, this is your best route to influencing change.

ISSUES IN IMPLEMENTATION

Until now, the approaches suggested to effect change have been about exerting powers of persuasion and relying on convincing colleagues

---

4.   www.bit.ly/2O8hEl3

of the veracity of your claims. Issues of policy, formal authority and power relations have not yet been considered. It is helpful at this point to consider two terms from legal discourse: 'de facto' and 'de jure'. The former relates to the facts on the ground: what the case is in actuality. The latter refers to the law, and how things should be ideally. For example, by law there can be no discrimination between people based on colour, sex, disability or creed.[5] De jure, that is the case. However, if one alleges that such discrimination takes place either by individuals or systems, they are arguing that it is not the case de facto. Returning to our school context, 'de facto' refers to what teachers actually do in their classroom, whereas 'de jure' refers to the policies which they are supposed to adhere to. Rarely, in my experience, do the two fully meet.

Of course, de facto and de jure realities have an effect on each other, usually mediated by consistency of implementation. If a school policy says that teachers should mark books once a fortnight but, as things turn out, nobody meets that target, strong leadership would re-evaluate the policy. The de facto reality would influence the de jure reality. If the school changed their policy to one featuring whole-class feedback then, with conditions discussed below, they might find that teachers' practices change: the de jure reality affects the de facto one.

Bringing in a policy and changing the de jure reality can cause changes in teacher activity, but only if it is implemented thoroughly. In general it is well known that whether it is implemented properly depends on monitoring and accountability, but a crucial factor which is often insufficiently acknowledged is how easy the policy actually is to implement. Some policies are incredibly difficult to implement, and regardless of the accountability that is attached to them, the de facto situation will never meet the ambition set de jure.

Let us take the simple example of implementing a low-stakes mini-quiz at the start of every lesson. As above, it is best to start by convincing people of the worth of regular retrieval practice.[6] But does that mean teachers actually get into the habit of carrying it out? I decided a number

---

5.   www.bit.ly/2tLLmFH
6.   www.bit.ly/2GtJcgx

of years ago that I wanted to start each lesson with a mini-quiz, but it took me 18 months before I actually managed to get into the habit of doing so. For any number of reasons, even if you have a team who all want to do a particular activity, it won't happen without a sensible policy and accompanying resources. A de jure policy that expects a mini-quiz every lesson and provides a resource by which to quickly and easily implement it will trump methods aimed at changing what people do de facto without recourse to a policy.

Pragmatically, sensible policies are ways to influence individuals and organisations who are opposing change for systemic reasons. They should not only remove old, ineffective practices, but they should also move evidence-informed, workload-reducing policies to the forefront of your team's minds. Realistically, they are a way to ensure that all students are being guaranteed a basic standard. If you have concerns about a particular teacher's performance, then in addition to your long-term coaching routes, a policy which ensures that all students are at least having regular retrieval will go towards ensuring a basic standard of quality for those students.

CONCLUSION

There is no general advice for implementing change that will work in all places at all times. It is vital that those who seek change carefully analyse and establish the nature of the forces standing in their way. Then, by tailoring their response to those forces they can, with any luck, help move our profession away from ineffective but 'appealing nostrums' (Carnine, 2000, p. 10) and towards a mature profession led by evidence, data, and the scientific method.

TOP TIPS:
- Start by establishing your opposition forces.
- Introduce your team to new ideas and broaden their ideas of what 'good' looks like.
- Recognise the difference between de jure and de facto realities (and how they influence each other) to clear away old, ineffective practices and policies and introduce new, effective and implementable ones.

REFERENCES

Bennett, T. and Boxer, A. (eds) (2019) *The researchED guide to explicit & direct instruction*. Woodbridge: John Catt Educational.

Boxer, A. (2018) 'In-school project: start a researchED reading group', *researchED* 2 (1) pp. 49–51. Retrieved from: www.bit.ly/2O7yznN [Accessed 18 November 2019].

Boxer, A. (2019) 'What is the best way to motivate students in your subject?', *Impact* 5. Retrieved from: www.bit.ly/2O8hEl3 [Accessed 17 November 2019].

Carnine, D. (2000) *Why education experts resist effective practices*. Washington, DC: Thomas B. Fordham Foundation.

Hazell, W. (2017) 'Exclusive: private university launches "first knowledge-based PGCE"', *Tes*, 21 July. Retrieved from: www.bit.ly/2O6WqEe [Accessed 17 November 2019].

ESTABLISHING AND SUSTAINING A MEANINGFUL CULTURE OF RESEARCH

LINDSAY PALMER *(@TheMeadTrust)*

Lindsay Palmer has worked as class teacher, SENCO and local authority advisor. Lindsay is currently the Head of Teaching School at The Mead Academy Trust, based in Trowbridge, Wiltshire. Since taking up this post, Lindsay has supported the development research-informed practice across Trust schools. Lindsay's research interests include effective approaches to professional development and evidence-based practice.

INTRODUCTION

The Mead Community Primary School began developing the use of research-informed practice more than seven years ago. The original aim was twofold:

1. to support staff to understand the nature and potential impact of engaging in research, and see themselves as practitioner researchers
2. to ensure that all professional development activity was evidence based and research informed, developing a culture of research engagement

The following chapter outlines how this approach was introduced and developed and how, as the academy trust grew, the approach was developed and extended from one school to three schools across the whole trust. Critically, this includes a focus on the conditions needed to establish a professional research culture and how this has become the foundation of a trust-wide approach to professional learning and a core strategy for school improvement.

Research-informed practice is now fundamental to trust development activity with all teachers and leaders actively research engaged. During the past few years, our approach has evolved from initial tentative steps to learning sets, research book clubs, teacher research groups, lesson study, research projects with the local authority and the leadership of an Education Endowment Foundation randomised controlled project. What we do is by no means a finished product. It is work in progress, aiming to fully embed a research-engaged approach throughout the trust.

INTRODUCING THE CONCEPT OF RESEARCH ENGAGEMENT

It was decided to use a teacher development day (teacher in-service training day) to explore the concept of research engagement more fully to staff. The training day was attended by all teaching and leadership staff (approximately 38). The day was planned in order to support all staff to gain a better understanding of research in the context of their own roles. Activities were designed carefully to consider the staff's wide range of experiences and qualifications and explore research concepts in ways to promote lively discussion and professional dialogue, including how research is used in the context of daily life, e.g. buying new shoes or a new computer.

Activities such as these enabled facilitators to gain a deeper understanding of the skills and attributes staff already possessed. It supported staff to see that they are, and can be, engaged in meaningful research activity, and that research is not an activity that belongs solely to 'white coated boffins in laboratories ... [and] unread impenetrable articles in esoteric journals' (Handscomb and MacBeath, 2003, p. 3). As the training day continued, colleagues were supported to understand that, in stark contrast to this stereotype, when schools and teachers are committed to research, it can be 'rooted in the day-to-day life of the classroom and the ongoing business of the school itself and its relationship with the community' (Handscomb, 2013).

During the latter part of the training day, the concept of learning sets (a collaborative group of teachers working together to undertake action research activity in a specific area) was introduced along with how these collaborative research groups would form the basis of development in key school improvement priority areas. Although the areas of focus were predetermined by school priorities, colleagues were able to choose which learning set to join. It was vital to the development of a valued research culture that colleagues were able to follow their own interests and be motivated by the research focus. A framework for action research was given to colleagues in order to support their thinking and research development. The framework supported the process of developing a research question, capturing baseline date, research methods and data collection. Colleagues were supported to develop research questions that were achievable, building on their own hunches that were integral to current classroom practice rather than additional to workload.

Over the course of the year, the learning sets continued to meet regularly, ensuring that the focus on enquiry-based practice was sustained so that disciplined innovation and collaborative enquiry were embedded and became the normal way of teaching and learning rather than the exception (BERA, 2014). The leadership team committed to allocating staff meetings, team meetings and further training days for learning set meetings to ensure that staff had dedicated time for this aspect of their work (Brown and Flood, 2019). The priority placed on this allocation of time supported the developing culture of research within the school and served to ensure additional workload for staff was minimised.

ESTABLISHING A CULTURE OF RESEARCH ENGAGEMENT

During the initial cycle of learning set research activity, the focus of the leadership team began to shift from simply supporting the group's ability to meet and progress, to considering how to make research approaches self-sustaining and impactful in the long term. The leadership team hoped to support colleagues to see how their own professional and pedagogical development and school development connected to research, literature and evidence. Leaders shared research summary documents and supported colleagues to consider their findings and how this could impact on decision making and school priorities. For example, aspects of the Education Endowment Foundation's *Teaching and Learning Toolkit* (2018) were examined and discussed in relation to learning set foci. In addition, well-known researchers and educationalists – such as Professor Steve Higgins and Pie Corbett – were invited to work with school staff at further training days.

Teachers were now interacting with research and evidence-based practice in several ways; for example: learning set research groups, current research documents and through listening to researchers in person. The impact of this approach placed research and evidence-based practice at the front and centre of all professional and pedagogical development.

As the learning sets began to near the end of their first cycle, focus shifted on to how best to disseminate and capture the results and impact of each group – what Stenhouse (1975) referred to as the 'importance of inquiry being made public'. A learning conference was planned for a teacher development day as a culmination to the learning set cycle. Each set would have a forum in which to share their work and outcomes. The day was also supported by Professor Graham Handscomb, who led a keynote address, in order that colleagues received external feedback and indeed validation, further embedding the importance and value of research. During the learning conference, learning sets were allocated a space within the school to display their research journey.

As expected from primary school teachers, the displays were amazingly creative and somewhat competitive! Over 70 staff attended the learning conference including teaching assistants (TAs). As a school the ambition was to include TAs into the next learning set cycle. It was felt important that the TAs understood what the teachers had been working on and how it related to practice development. Staff visited all of the displays and had opportunities to discuss outcomes and impact with group members.

Learning set leads produced a case study of their group's research, outcomes and impact. These were published on the school and teaching school websites and informed school development and policy. For example, the five-point scale (Dunn and Curtis, 2012) considered during one set continues to be a fundamental part of not only The Mead School's behaviour policy but also now across all the trust's schools. The school and trust have adapted the five-point scale framework in order to support whole-school, group and individual pupil behaviour.

The first cycle of learning sets led to demonstrable impact on school development and practice. Teachers appeared to understand how research and evidence-based practice could be used to good effect on personal and whole-school development. A culture of research had certainly been established, but it was now vital to sustain and develop this further.

EMBEDDING A CULTURE OF RESEARCH ENGAGEMENT

Through feedback and discussion, leaders identified the key aspects of activities undertaken to date that had contributed positively to the successful development of a research culture within school. These included:

- Research foci being contextually relevant and practically useful and linking explicitly to school development leading directly to knowledge creation (Stoll, 2008)
- Practitioners being able to direct their own thinking and research based on hunches and interests, supported by leaders

- Practitioners being involved in not only their own research but the research of others
- Prioritising time and resources to enable practitioners to dedicate quality time to research activity and dissemination (Brown and Flood, 2019)

However, leaders were aware that the concept of research engagement needed to be kept at the forefront of thinking without it losing its appeal to staff. With that in mind, during the past seven years a range of strategies and activities have been undertaken to maintain and further develop focus and interest.

A second cycle of learning sets was undertaken for teaching staff. The foci were once again driven by school improvement priorities. In parallel to this, teaching assistants also took part in their own learning sets. A joint dissemination event was held which enabled both teachers and TAs to share their research journeys and outcomes. A short time after the second learning set cycle, The Mead Primary School was joined by two further primary schools, forming The Mead Academy Trust. Trust leaders were determined to embed research engagement across the trust and within each school but also collaboratively across the schools. The leadership team recognised that this had to be balanced alongside other key development needs within the schools. As such, it was decided that only members of the middle and senior leadership teams within the new schools would take part in research activity alongside staff at The Mead. The aim was for these members of staff to become 'research champions' in their own schools. In addition, all staff at the new schools joined training and development activities which continued to have a strong evidence-based, research-engaged focus. In this way, research engagement and activity became part of professional dialogue in the new schools raising its profile in a less formalised way, ensuring staff became familiar with the 'language' of research and its impact on practice first hand.

Over the following year or so, engagement in research activity expanded to include more and more staff across the three schools. The trust is now in a position where all teachers are engaging in teacher research groups (TRGs). A conscious decision was made to rename the research groups 'TRGs' instead of 'learning sets' in order for the whole trust to have ownership of the name, rather than simply viewing the activity as something that had been inherited from one of the schools. The TRGs are now fully established and membership consists of staff from all three schools (schools are geographically a maximum of 15 minutes apart by car, and as such cross-school meetings are easy to manage). The value given to the groups continues to be demonstrated, firstly by a commitment to shared staff meetings across the schools to enable groups to meet and secondly by dedicated meeting time during teacher development days. The TRGs now focus on shared trust-wide priorities. Recent groups have considered nurtured learning provision, the use of journaling techniques in maths, assessment and feedback in writing and reading approaches in key stage 2. There has been demonstrable impact on teaching and learning approaches, including the implementation of a whole-class feedback approach and the publication of guidance related to the use of journaling.

Dissemination approaches have also developed and have been streamlined. TRGs are now asked to complete an academic poster to delineate their research question, journey and outcomes, rather than writing longer time-consuming case studies. These will be shared both internally and externally. There continues to be demonstrable impact on pedagogy and approaches across all trust schools as a result of research activity. For example, last year one TRG considered feedback and marking and as a result developed a new approach to whole-class marking that was piloted. This is now a fundamental part of marking across all trust schools and has impacted significantly on reducing teacher workload.

Research activity has had a fundamental impact on teaching and learning, including the development of new or revised approaches to marking, assessment and feedback, planning, and specific teaching approaches such as the use of manipulatives in maths. The value given to research-based activity by staff across the trust has become so high that the nature and reach of activity has been developed further.

- A number of staff have been involved in the management and development of a randomised control trial with the Education Endowment Foundation (EEF); a two-year funded project to develop, trial and implement a maths intervention programme (www.mathscounts.co.uk). This enabled a number of staff to be involved in a much larger formal randomised control trial, supporting the development of their understanding of research methodology. The project resulted in the Maths Counts intervention project being revised and further established within trust schools and beyond. A significant number of children at risk of underachievement have now been supported through the programme.
- In some of the trust schools, staff have developed their own research 'book clubs'. A book is chosen and is read and discussed over an agreed period of time. Staff have valued the opportunity to reflect on their reading and engage in professional dialogue. Texts have been linked to keynote speakers at training days or to school and trust development priorities. Staff have told the leadership team that they would have been unlikely to engage with this type of literature had the book club not existed.
- Teachers from all trust schools are now also engaged in lesson study. The trust was lucky enough to be supported by colleagues from Three Bridges Primary School in Southall, London to introduce this model. Staff from Three Bridges sat alongside senior leaders from The Mead Trust for the first lesson study week. This supported staff from The Mead to take the model forward and develop it further. The Mead Trust is now committed to each year group from across the trust working together at least once per year on a focused lesson study week. This includes releasing all staff from teaching commitments in order to fully engage. Thus far, the focus of the lesson study has been on maths teaching. There is demonstrable impact on teaching and learning in maths as a result of this approach. All lesson study activity is recorded for internal use and published externally on websites.
- Teachers from across the trust took part in a DfE-funded research project relating to workload (supported by Professor Graham

Handscomb). This project explored the role of subject specialists in the development of planning and resulted in significant changes being made to planning approaches, which impacted significantly on teacher workload (Handscomb et al., 2017).

CONCLUSION

If you were to ask staff across the academy trust about the role research plays in the development of the school, the trust and their own practice, I am confident their answers would be emphatically positive. Research and evidence-based practice is 'who we are' and 'what we do'. Staff are supported to be engaged 'with' and equipped to engage 'in' enquiry-orientated practice, which BERA (2014) suggests teachers need in order to be at their most effective. Research activity is now woven into everyday practice and all aspects of professional development. Indeed, even the term 'professional development' is no longer used in order to try to convey a more person-centred and individual approach, instead being replaced by the term 'professional growth'. Appraisal documentation values research engagement for both teachers and teaching assistants and there is an expectation that engagement in research activity is part of these roles (see figure 1 overleaf as an example).

Seven years ago, one school set out to implement a more research-based approach to school and staff professional development. It has not been a smooth journey. It has needed a huge amount of commitment from leadership at all levels including the allocation of time and resources. Expanding the approach from a single school to a multi-academy trust of three presented significant challenge. It took time and patience to develop the model to work effectively within the new context. However, when reflecting on the past few years, it is clear that the trust has moved from an approach to professional learning that relied on 'explicit rational discovery' to one that relies on 'tacit rational discovery', that truly values individual input and that encourages collective discourse and collegial support (Palmer, 2004). As Aristotle suggests, 'collective deliberation by the many is always preferable to the isolated deliberation of the individual' (Carr, 1998, p. 71). The journey will of course never

Teachers' Standards –	Emerging Teachers	Accomplished Teachers	Expert Teachers		
Part 1	MPS 1/2	MPS 3/4	MPS 5/6	UPS 1/2	UPS 3
Demonstrate a critical understanding of developments in the subject and curriculum areas, and promote the value of scholarship	Sound awareness of the developments in subjects and curriculum areas in own year group and ability to adapt teaching when necessary to ensure latest requirements are met. Take responsibility for own learning and development through attending staff training and events and reading current literature and research. Take an active role in action research and lesson study.	Secure awareness of developments in subjects and curriculum areas in and beyond own year group. Be research engaged, source relevant information and take advantage of opportunities to develop own practice. Take an increasingly active role in research activity, taking the lead on occasion. Share information with colleagues.	Critical understanding of subjects and curriculum areas in and beyond own year group. Support, mentor and coach colleagues to model and share developing ideas and good practice. Independently research and pilot new initiatives in own class and across the year group/phase. Take an increasing lead in whole-school research activity.	Monitor and evaluate colleagues' knowledge and understanding of curriculum initiatives and innovation to improve provision across the school. Active engagement in research and enquiry. Model the value of scholarship and professional development across the school. Lead action research and lesson study to ensure that the school is at the forefront of innovative and engaging subject and curriculum developments.	Monitor, evaluate and analyse colleagues' knowledge and understanding of curriculum initiatives and innovation to ensure improvements are made across the trust. Demonstrate an active engagement in research and enquiry, modelling the value of scholarship and professional development across the trust. Lead research into new curriculum-wide initiatives to ensure that the trust is at the forefront of innovative and engaging subject and curriculum developments.

Figure 1 – Extract from 'Teacher Appraisal Handbook' (Palmer, 2018)

end. Approaches and process require continual reviewing in the light of current school and trust contexts to ensure they remain fit for purpose and impactful.

TOP TIPS

When reflecting on the past seven years of research engagement, there are a number of aspects that have been key to its success and long-term sustainability and would be recommended for any school or trust wanting to implement a culture of research engagement and practice:

- **Develop a culture of research.** Focus on a whole-school approach that will impact on everyone. Take time to ensure all staff are involved and understand the nature of research engagement and what it means for them. It needs to be an attainable approach, not something that just academics do and that is removed from everyday classroom practice. Know your staff and find those who have some understanding of research activity and use them as 'champions' for the approach.
- **Start from personal interests.** When implementing a first venture into research activity, enable staff to explore their personal interests and hypotheses where possible. As with any new initiative, focusing on current interests sparks curiosity and engagement. Experience at The Mead shows that even the most sceptical of staff saw value when the starting points were directly affecting their own practice and interests. The success of the first research activity is vital for securing its long-term sustainability.
- **Provide time and resources.** A full commitment from leaders is needed to effectively embed research engagement. In order for research activity to be part and parcel of professional practice, it needs to be given the same priority as other areas of practice and thus needs clear time commitment for staff meetings and training days. Experience at The Mead shows emphatically that, as a result of research engagement teacher, workload can be decreased. However, it is vital that the actual act of researching does not add to workload.

REFERENCES

BERA (2014) *Research and the teaching profession: building the capacity for a self-improving education system.* BERA: London.

Brown, C. and Flood, J. (2019) *Formalise, prioritise and mobilise: how school leaders secure the benefits of professional learning networks.* London: Emerald.

Carr, W. (1998) *For education: towards critical educational inquiry.* Buckingham: Open University Press.

Dunn, K. and Curtis, M. (2012) *The incredible 5-point scale: the significantly improved and expanded second edition.* Shawnee, KS: AAPC.

Education Endowment Foundation (2018) *Teaching and Learning Toolkit* [Online]. Retrieved from www.bit.ly/2RUkdZ6 [Accessed 30 October 2019].

Handscomb, G. (2013) 'Making research make a difference in the classroom', *SecEd* [Online], 26 September. Retrieved from: www.bit.ly/39RMsz0 [Accessed 30 October 2019].

Handscomb, G. and MacBeath, J. (2003) *The research engaged school.* Chelmsford: Essex County Council.

Handscomb, G., Palmer, L., Couzens, S. and Cunningham, R. (2017) Collaborate, plan and renew: reducing workload and increasing confidence through curriculum planning. Department for Education. London: The Stationery Office.

Palmer, L. (2004) 'Evaluating a new model of in-service education and training' [Master's dissertation].

Palmer, L. (2018) 'Teacher appraisal handbook'. Trowbridge: The Mead Academy Trust.

Stenhouse, L. (1975) *An introduction to curriculum research and development.* London: Heinemann.

Stoll, L. (2008) 'Leadership and policy learning communities: promoting knowledge animation' in Chakroun, B. and Sahlberg, P. (eds) *ETF yearbook 2008: policy learning in action.* Turin: European Training Foundation, pp. 107–112.

RETHINKING RESEARCH
USING INSET TO GROW A RESEARCH-ACTIVE CULTURE

MARCELLA McCARTHY *(mccarthy.education@gmail.com)*

Dr Marcella McCarthy was a University Lecturer for ten years before moving into secondary education, and has since worked with a wide range of primary and secondary schools on teaching and learning. She is currently Deputy Head at the Royal Latin School in Buckingham and has written two books for Bloomsbury: *The Spider Strategy and Mentoring and Coaching.*

INTRODUCTION

Ask most teachers what they understand by active research and their replies make it sound formidable. People speak about taking on MAs, or training to do their NPQML or NPQH. Sometimes they mention being part of a larger research project outside school. Research is often seen as time-consuming or only for the ambitious teacher seeking promotion. For a profession which is time-poor, under pressure and under stress, it's therefore not a priority.

And yet research is enriching. If you speak to teachers who have engaged in research, they are enthusiastic about the ways in which it has made their teaching better. They talk about the impact that it makes to take time out from the spinning wheel of work, and the ways in which it has allowed them to reflect on other aspects of practice. They talk about how it has re-enthused them about their subject. Speaking once to

51

a senior colleague about this, he said, 'Yes, I'd like to send everyone out to do an MA.' Sadly, it was a joke; many schools have had to cut CPD budgets for all but exam-related courses, and staff wellbeing has suffered as a result.

But despite this gloomy picture, we don't need to pine after MAs (which might not be the right thing for everyone in any case). Every year, after all, teachers have five days which should be specifically dedicated to training: in-service training (INSET) days. INSET days can sometimes be less than inspiring. Moving from university to secondary teaching, I found it extraordinary to sit through a powerpoint being read out slowly to explain to us all how to teach more excitingly. Coming from an environment where, as a matter of normal expectation, teaching was informed by research – and what you discovered today, you might be teaching to students tomorrow – I felt as if the pace and energy that I had enjoyed in university teaching was sometimes diluted, and that INSET days were often wasted time. How to use INSET days more productively – how to claim back at least some of that time to create a research culture – has been the subject of my personal research project over the past year and a half.

RETHINKING WHAT WE MEAN BY RESEARCH

There are many problems with embedding research-based practice in schools. Firstly, research is often seen as something that happens away from the 'real world' of classroom management. Secondly, connected to this, there can be a tendency to think that research is irrelevant – a view so ingrained that sites such as *Teacher Toolkit* even have 'mythbuster' sections to try to defend research-based practice. Thirdly, it's likely that people are going to see research as 'one more thing' to do that militates against the dreaded twin priorities of budget and results and saps wellbeing. Because of this, there's a real danger that promoting research-based practice in a school can turn into just another version of the 'hero head' approach, where the impetus for change comes from the top down, and not the bottom up. To be meaningful, research needs to arise out of the everyday context in which a school works, and also has to have an impact and relevance for the school itself.

At the Royal Latin School, we wanted to encourage a climate where people worked in community, shared ideas across subjects, and engaged in active research. We also wanted to encourage staff wellbeing. We therefore moved towards creating a research-active school in stages, using INSET days to facilitate a move from leader-led research – where you're getting people to try out or implement what you believe will work – to teacher-led research – where people are putting into practice their own findings, reading for themselves, and engaging in active and independent research.

To start with, we encouraged staff to see the ways in which, as teachers, they are all researchers already. A reflective practitioner who teaches a lesson and then revises it in order to deliver it to a different group is participating in a form of research, albeit not one which may be written up in a journal. Someone teaching a new text or topic who goes away to read about it before teaching is also engaging in research. Every time you try something new (that, for example, you heard about on Twitter) in the classroom, you are evaluating its impact; every time you notice the effect that a strategy has, and decide that you will use it again, you are implementing the fruits of your research.

By fostering this approach, in the course of just over a year, we have moved from being a school where 86.6% of staff said that they would like to use INSET days simply 'to prepare for the term ahead' to a school where on our last INSET day every teacher engaged in an individual piece of research, valuable to them and valuable to the school. 93.3% of staff have said that they believe that this experience will lead them to pursue further active research, and 100% of staff have asked to repeat the experience in future INSET days.

It's only a first step; nonetheless, this is how we did it.

OPENING OUT THE IDEA OF RESEARCH

In order to model for staff how research could be brought into practice, we decided to focus an INSET session last year upon the issue of boys' achievement: it was a school priority to try to improve boys' progress, which had lagged behind that of girls. The session commenced with a presentation of the facts and research about how boys and girls achieve in different areas, including a spot of 'mythbusting', which raised some of the different ways of thinking about the topic. We asked staff to consider whether they thought there was an inherent difference in the ways that boys and girls learn, and introduced them to some of the research that addressed the issue.

By sitting staff in cross-curricular groups, facilitated by a member of staff who was *not* a middle or senior leader (though all staff participated in the groups), we encouraged them to discuss the input with people not in their own subject area. We kept them in these groups to compare books across subjects, encouraging discussion about how learning looked in *our* school, in *our* context. Each group had in it at least one person we knew would have the potential to act as a catalyst for others, and the topic provoked lively debate.

Each group of staff was then asked to commit to a plan working with the people in their group over the following term. Various possibilities were suggested: to visit each other's lessons and focus on a specific area of practice; to track a particular student or group of students; to explore a hypothesis about learning in your different subject areas; to do a joint learning walk or even to plan a small research project. Staff were encouraged to try strategies that took little time. One popular suggestion was a 'plenary swap', where teachers visit the last 15 minutes of each other's lessons. Another was a 'marking locum' where staff swap and mark a set of books. Staff were given freedom as to the nature of the project, but a focus on boys' achievement as a whole-school priority was encouraged.

The training got some very positive responses; people were excited and interested by the idea of looking closely at a whole-school issue, and happy to go and watch others teach. Feeding back as a part of the next INSET day, we discovered that using boys' achievement as a 'hook' had been helpful in that it gave staff immediate ideas about possible lines of enquiry. We had some wonderful outcomes, including musicians and scientists comparing how they dealt with practical work, and humanities teachers watching PE staff to find out about how to develop more effective questioning. As the year went on, people further developed their projects, and we started to see real impact. Interest grew. Boys' achievement become something that people talked about, and argued about, and discussed when they were looking at teaching and learning. It might be a coincidence that in that summer's GCSEs, with all results improved, boys nonetheless achieved higher than girls in both progress and attainment – but it felt like a consequence.

TRYING NEW THINGS

With a lot of positive comments from staff about the research projects that they had commenced, it was the negative comments that were the most helpful in planning our next steps. Although many staff were ready to become research active, a smaller number did not really want to get involved, seeing it as a distraction from their main work. Having started the research conversation, we felt that the next stage was to enquire in more depth about what people wanted and expected from their training. In other words, the conversation had been started, but there was still a lot to do.

Google Forms was invaluable for this part of the research: it produces instant charts and diagrams to display results, and allowed us to combine multiple-choice questioning with longer and more reflective written answers. We quickly found that there was a demand from staff for input and expertise from outside, but also a new hunger to work independently and start their own research.

Amongst the positive outcomes that came from the research focus was that a number of people wanted to start working parties in different areas. One group specifically didn't want to be involved with any school-based projects, but nonetheless determined to meet at regular intervals to discuss different pieces of research. One head of department started a new feature of department meetings where colleagues were given an article or book section to look at and reflect on, and then tell people about at the next meeting – it was a huge success, and led to lots of new strategies being trialled.

A significant thing that we noticed coming up again and again in the feedback was how much people enjoyed having more autonomy about what they did in INSET time. We therefore trialled some 'carousel' sessions, based on the priorities which we had identified through questionnaires, on the next INSET day. People were able to spend some time attending sessions which were specifically tailored to their interests and needs, and some of our most enthusiastic researchers were also able to share good practice. Feedback from these sessions was extremely positive (87% of staff rating them good or excellent); however, we wanted to try something even more innovative which would encourage the research culture further.

LIFT-OFF: AN INDEPENDENT STAFF RESEARCH DAY

What we decided on finally was nothing more or less than to trust staff. We were fortunate to have an INSET day that was at the end of the autumn half term, and which did not coincide with INSET days at other local schools. Staff had been asking to visit other schools, and to visit universities as well. We had been encouraging them to read research and felt that the time was right to develop further. As a result, we assigned our INSET day as an independent staff research day. Staff were told that they could use it for any research purpose, whether that was to visit another school to work with colleagues there, to visit a university or place of work connected to their subject specialism, or to do some independent reading. We especially encouraged research relating to their subject area because part of the feedback we had been given had suggested that this was an area often neglected in INSETs that focus on pedagogy.

We asked staff to let us know about their plans in advance (and any support that they wished for, such as facilitating contact with different institutions). They had a certain amount of freedom – for instance, the day could be taken in lieu if an activity was undertaken at a weekend, or at another time during half term – but whatever they chose to do, they had to write a report on it as part of the day. They were encouraged to take time to reflect, but in the event we found people actually working for longer than on an ordinary INSET day, because they were energised and enthused.

Reporting back on the specific projects undertaken on the day is beyond the remit of this chapter but staff took part in a far wider range of activities than expected. They travelled long distances to visit universities that specialised in a particular subject area; they worked with tertiary colleagues at the university next door; they set up active research with other schools; they attended conferences; they went to work with experts such as those at the RSC; they attended specific training in a specialist area; they investigated new discoveries in their subject area.

A striking element of the feedback was the extent to which teachers felt that it had had an immediate impact on their practice. Comments made by staff reflect this sense of relevance: 'Since undertaking the training, I have already made use of the new skills gained to aid my teaching. The skills learnt have improved my efficiency and are applicable across all key stages'; 'The research I did has shown me ways in which I have failed to take account of previous research; I am saving myself time'; 'I have lots of ideas that I want to discuss further and implement in the school'; 'I am able to use my research directly in my teaching and sharing that practice with the department. I loved doing it.'

What we also noticed was the sheer positivity that came with the freedom to explore and research beyond school, as you can see from the word cloud created from the feedback. All staff rated the day as 'very good' (20%) or 'excellent' (80%), and 98.1% of staff reported that they believed the day would have a positive impact on their future work. As one member of staff said, 'This has been the most productive INSET I have had in my career! Good for professional development *and* wellbeing.'

TOP TIPS:

- **Endorse and encourage the research that is done every day in the classroom.** Many people don't identify what they do as research, although often the difference is simply that they're not writing it up. In the same way, people don't always see keeping up to date on the latest work in their specialism as 'research', although it is immensely valuable for teachers.

- **Don't be afraid; trying something new is the essence of research.** Getting it 'wrong' is also a valuable lesson. If research teaches us anything it is that we test hypotheses – we don't simply seek to reinforce our existing bias. If one idea for building up research doesn't fly, don't despair – just learn from it.
- **Ask staff what they need, and** trust them. Each school is different, but most teachers are highly committed, hardworking professionals. It is crucial for their wellbeing and development that they have some autonomy in their professional development. One of the words that came back again and again in our positive feedback was 'trust'.

COGNITION CREW – NAVIGATING OUR WAY THROUGH RESEARCH AS A TRUST

'A SMOOTH SEA NEVER MADE A SKILFUL SAILOR'

HANNA MILLER (*@notesfromthebun*)

Hanna Miller is Assistant Headteacher for teaching and learning at Gordon Children's Academy and also has a multi-academy trust role for teaching and learning which oversees 17 primary and secondary schools across Kent, Medway and Portsmouth.

WHAT DOES IT MEAN TO BE RESEARCH INFORMED IN OUR TRUST?

Teaching is a complex business. Despite this, we are fortunate enough as a profession to have an increasingly strong consensus about what effective teaching 'looks like' in the classroom, and bridging the gap between academia and school practice is becoming more of a focus in our field. Organisations like the Education Endowment Foundation are engaging teachers with distillations of evidence and findings to allow them to make better-informed decisions about what goes on in their classrooms.

Teaching will never be a clear science – some would consider it a craft but research within education can provide us with clarity over where and the extent to which there is consensus, so that we can use this evidence to inform decisions to ensure that what we do in the classroom is more likely to have a positive impact. Research will not secure these decisions but ensure that we are not basing decisions on intuition alone.

As Wiliam (2016) states, 'everything works somewhere but nothing works everywhere'. Our staff in the trust are therefore encouraged to critically consume research and ask, 'Under what conditions might this work?' when looking at solutions to improve classroom practice. The key word here being 'might' – implying that schools are multifaceted ecosystems that require one to honour the context when considering the implications of research. Time and energy spent looking for silver bullets is wasted when we should be focusing more on what effective practice looks like in our schools for our children. To do this successfully, we must be mentally agile, just as athletes hoping to outwit opponents on the sports field need to be agile – changing direction quickly whilst maintaining balance. The same applies to us as educators: we need to always remain balanced – balanced in terms of considering research with a dual focus: on what might support but also on what might contradict in our own settings. Without this balance, it is too easy to fall into a trap of being research led, changing direction and likely failing.

When introducing new concepts or attempting to solve problems, I carefully structure staff discussions to invite dialogue along the lines of the examples below to support colleagues in exercising criticality and making more secure decisions to inform their practice:

- 'Research findings suggest that ... And this is important to us because...'
- 'This might mean ... for our children/school so let's consider ... because...'
- 'But be mindful of ... because...'
- 'So an important message here is ... and in my classroom that might mean I need to...'

It is a big ask to suggest that all teachers need to be researchers or actively engage in research but colleagues do need to value the role that research plays within the profession and how we can use it to inform our decisions. This became my priority – understanding how to distil lots of research into something that was digestible for staff.

One of the biggest challenges across a multi-academy trust is how to effectively scale down findings of research to meet the needs of varying contexts, whilst also scaling up effective practice from individual classrooms or schools to ensure that all our students have the same chance to achieve the best educational outcomes. An additional challenge that evolves from this is the balance between opportunity and cost. As leaders in education, we need to consider the impact of encouraging our teachers to be research informed. If we value the role of research in the school and wish practitioners to base decisions on strong foundations, then we need to think carefully about where that time is coming from, and as a result what we might be leaving behind.

LEARNING HOW TO NAVIGATE THE SEAS
Creative professional development

Continuing professional development (CPD) can involve a whole range of activities, spanning informal conversations with colleagues during break time to attendance at formal conferences. In particular I am aligned with Day (1999, p. 4) in suggesting an all- encompassing definition of CPD as:

> 'the process by which, alone and with others, teachers review, renew and extend their commitment as change agents to the moral purposes of teaching; and by which they acquire and develop critically the knowledge, skills and emotional intelligence essential to good professional thinking, planning and practice.'

How much of our time designated to professional development is spent reviewing and renewing? How empowered do we feel to be a change agent? How do we effectively develop criticality and emotional intelligence to inform practice? The approach we have used within our trust is to provide an extended CPD offer in the form of 'Cognition Crew' – a termly, voluntary, evening event designed to upskill staff in a non-conformist, zero-accountability low-stakes format. Similar to a journal club, all colleagues – teachers and support staff – are invited to discuss the applications of group-selected guidance reports, articles, book chapters or reports that they found particularly interesting. These selected pieces are usually chosen by previous attendees and go to an online vote, enabling us to select where the majority lies. This helps to secure commitment whilst also providing an opportunity for professional dialogue with other like-minded colleagues.

All schools are encouraged to send a representative, but as the club runs in the evening and is not part of directed hours, I am happy for it to remain a group of committed individuals who attend because they want to discuss readings, share understandings and practise their skills of 'intellectual interrogation'. They are sent the study piece beforehand to read and annotate and then attend the evening meet with colleagues from across the trust. There is a consistent group of approximately 20 attendees.

The original intent was to encourage more staff to engage with different forms of research which would then aid their understanding, meaning that research could be more purposefully used and those staff would then hopefully make better decisions in their classrooms. Attendees would feel part of the group and as a result feel more confident sharing their theories and interpretations back at their own schools because they have used the opportunity to 'test the waters' within the group. In this way, Cognition Crew was developing a community which offered a safe space to discuss ideas prior to actioning them, rather than a team of lone rangers.

The development of questioning minds is a core theme of Cognition Crew – the expectation is not to attend the meet already having digested and fully understood the paper but to have chewed it over and attend with some questions. By the time we have unpicked the paper as a group, we should be asking ourselves 'Are we doing the best we can?' and 'Are there better alternatives?' These guiding questions link directly to each of our schools and the subjects and year groups that we teach and they form a safe way to 'intellectually interrogate', where we refine each other's ideas and viewpoints professionally. There are no formal rules of Cognition Crew but a professional approach to questioning and debate is expected. This quality collaboration relies on a symbiotic relationship between own values, findings from research, context of the school and direction of the trust. This requires collegiate trust, support and an empathetic approach to problem solving – all features that are nurtured in the style of Cognition Crew. It is a choice to attend and we all aim to leave taking more from the table than we individually brought.

The benefits of Cognition Crew

What I have most enjoyed about Cognition Crew is the positive impact it has had on my own practice. I've always been someone who would choose to engage with research in my own time, but Cognition Crew has the added benefit that it is situated within our context. I'm discussing ideas with people who teach the same students and have the same school pressures and perceived constraints, which makes those discussions more purposeful. I too have explored, trialled, monitored and shared findings from Cognition Crew in my own classroom. For me, this was a method to model and help support less established or experienced staff to think about how interventions can work; but for others it was to provide confidence. Many attendees have commented that Cognition Crew has given them a licence to explore – confidence to seek out what is 'working' and methods to intervene appropriately.

Cognition Crew is not to test knowledge but to discuss interpretations, strengths of research sources, possible limitations and possible applications to own context. A committed core set of staff attending consistently feed back new thinking and knowledge to their own schools and this provides a vehicle for improving the quality of discussions around teaching in schools. This form of commitment goes far beyond connecting and networking.

Sharing knowledge and practice

Some members of Cognition Crew have in the past prepared a 'distilled read' for colleagues from their own schools as a way of sharing the information from the evening, which also serves to consolidate their own thinking. On no more than an A4 page, they outlined what the research stated, summarised some of our group discussion points and provided examples of how the research might be relevant to practice at their school. These would then be sent to staff members in their home school and often referred to in brief sections of staff meetings or professional development sessions – providing those unable to attend with a voice too.

If the messages are not fed back to schools formally through 'distilled reads', practice and ideas are disseminated through informal discussions whilst photocopying, waiting for the kettle to boil or passing down the corridor. These informal methods are sometimes more significant in that they are based around a virtuous circle – they depend on those connections between staff but also strengthen them too. And what makes them richer is that these connections know no hierarchy – it's just people influencing circles of practice with what has come from the discussions with colleagues; these are not directives.

With the approach now in its third year, each Cognition Crew session remains voluntary. Governors from the trust and colleagues from other trusts and schools have also attended sessions to provide the necessary alternative perspectives. These 'critical friends' (Swaffield, 2004) prevent our meetings from becoming echo chambers and allow us to remain critical and cautious of being too certain.

Cognition Crew has also supported the development of cross-school collaborations – for example, as a result of the session looking into the EEF report on marking, three of the secondary school English staff shared a small project into whole-class feedback. This could have happened without Cognition Crew but it was self-developed and so from the start had more commitment and interest.

A further notable development correlating to the Cognition Crew movement has been that more teachers are closely monitoring their practice and are not just doing what they do out of habit or because it's what they've been told to do; they are actively becoming informed about their decisions, taking ownership of their research diet and becoming 'critical consumers' of research.

Professional learning
In addition, there have been developments in the language and activities we choose to use to engage staff in professional learning within school. The connotations of professional development can sometimes be negative

and reminiscent of a 'done to' model of learning rather than a research-informed professional learning journey. Continuing professional development (CPD) has been renamed 'continuing professional learning' (CPL) to acknowledge the cyclical nature of exploring, integrating, embedding and innovating rather than purely identifying weaknesses and developing. While this might seem a small change in language, it represents a big change in focus, format and value to reflect the movement towards integrating more research findings to inform our decisions in school. High-quality CPL in the workplace is an entitlement for all staff and the movement to 'learning' from 'development' suggests that trialling and exploring is OK – it is important to work out the conditions under which research is applicable.

As a direct result of the wider reading taking place in Cognition Crew, my school has moved towards an almost flipped-learning approach to CPL where a pre-reading is provided a week before the CPL session. Flipped learning is sometimes appropriate for teaching students in the classroom; and in our case, where staff have access to time and space to pre-read, it involves instructional content being introduced prior to the CPL – a hyperlink sent via email for ease of access and then followed up on and applied within the CPL. Staff have the choice to read this in their own time or they can arrive to the CPL session ten minutes early and engage with the piece. After each CPL, staff are encouraged to share their takeaways and successes in their classrooms. We have also been trialling purpose-built 'drop in' proformas which summarise the research shared in the CPL in two or three bullet points, give examples of what it looks like in classrooms, and provide questions to consider for own practice and a small space to self- or peer-reflect. This distillation into a workable A4 sheet condenses down the important points and allows staff to ensure their decisions and takeaways are accurate and purposeful.

Making an impact

Staff are also strongly encouraged to focus their targets on where their current successes lie. Often in education we can run what look like deficit models – filling the gap, identifying the weakness – but in some cases success breeds motivation. If we can identify what is effective and use research to inform a tweak in teaching practice – a marginal gain – then over time that means greater outcomes across all aspects of teaching. And these marginal gains are about finding the 'one per cents'. These small changes in classroom practice over time can add up to huge impacts (Buck, 2018). Just the notion of one per cent is motivating to staff because you are looking at something manageable – it doesn't hold connotations of excessive workload demands. The system of staff self-selecting their areas of focus has also provided an increased ownership of how practice in their subject and year groups develops, which in turn breeds a deeper commitment to growth and research use.

Each school has an assigned drive team leader to support staff with these research-informed decisions but also support the dissemination of research within each school. The drive team leader attends regular group meetings with other drive team leaders across the trust to discuss strengths, areas for concern and solutions in a 'problem-solving team-building protocol' approach. This approach enables colleagues to recognise the expertise present within a group of highly skilled practitioners.

The language and application of ideas will develop as our understanding of cognitive science and education-based research develops and evolves – research updates and new findings will provide opportunities to revisit what we think we know and ensure we meet the needs of the students within our trust and support our teachers to be the best they can be. As these developments occur, we adjust our sails to keep our same course to be the best we can be.

It is not about working harder or longer but about working smarter. The staff that attend these events are not just those who have carved out time in their diaries; they are skilful sailors in an unpredictable sea, working in complex areas to come together to keep the ship sailing in the right direction. School improvement is sometimes like turning a ship – it takes time and effort and is about incremental gains – those one per cents.

The expertise and drive to really transform the lives of our students through a research-informed process grows when given the space and time to flourish.

TOP TIPS

- Keep criticality at the heart of everything – surround yourselves with people who think differently to keep criticality present.
- Provide at least one member of staff with access to an online research bank to support those looking for articles. Don't kill engagement with pay walls to quality research.
- Demonstrate where possible how much you value research-informed practice by extending the CPD offer to include events like Cognition Crew.

REFERENCES

Buck, A. (2018) *Leadership matters 3.0*. Woodbridge: John Catt Educational.

Day, C. (1999) *Developing teachers: the challenges of lifelong learning*. London: Falmer Press.

Swaffield, S. (2004) 'Critical friends: supporting leadership, improving learning', *Improving Schools* 7 (3) pp. 267–278.

Wiliam, D. (2016) *Leadership for teacher learning*. West Palm Beach, FL: Learning Sciences International.

OVERCOMING TEACHERS' RESERVATIONS AND BARRIERS
TO ENGAGING WITH EDUCATIONAL RESEARCH

CLAIRE HARLEY (*@clairevharley*)

Claire Harley is a history teacher and Head of Department. In a previous role Claire worked as Research Lead and Senior Leader responsible for teaching, learning and innovation. Her EdD research at the University of Nottingham explores teachers' and leaders' perceptions of research-informed practice.

There has been a notable shift towards research engagement in schools. Exponentially, charities, universities, academics, consultants, teaching schools and other external organizations have declared support for the use of educational research in schools. The pursuit of research-informed practice can positively support the teaching profession and should be encouraged (Brown et al., 2018), but how can this be achieved? Who should be included in the pursuit of research informed teaching remains a point of contention. The role of policymakers and school leaders in evidence-based education is causing some to call into question what we really mean by evidence (Biesta, 2010). Within the education system, there is a voice of dissent that does not accept the need for research-engaged practice. We may not hear them on platforms such as 'EduTwitter', but if we go into the staffroom after briefing (when SLT have left) we will hear the occasional groan and the conversation between busy teachers who simply ask one another when they will have the time to implement this or that.

This chapter approaches the topic of research-informed practice as a potential force for good in teachers' practice. For me, it links back to my favourite quote by essayist Ralph Waldo Emerson: 'I cannot remember the books I've read any more than the meals I have eaten; even so, they have made me.' Imagine the potential of an education system where each adult who comes into contact with children makes decisions based on a wealth of knowledge; where practice is improved by informing practitioners' thinking (Cain et al., 2019). There are, however, educators who do not identity research as part of their work. Before we look at the barriers and reservations teachers have about engaging with educational research, I think it is important to state that many of these concerns are legitimate. Rather than seeing our less enthused colleagues as old fashioned, uncommitted or unacademic, we remember that progress is much more likely to be authentic and entrenched if all feel valued and listened to as part of the process. If anything, there is room for a level of healthy cynicism; the critical eye can be a welcome barrier to the implementation of gimmicks or time-consuming and ineffectual policies. Research-informed practice highlights the issues surrounding the motivations and justifications school leaders use as part of their decision-making process. As such, the need for trust between teachers, school leaders and policy makers is magnified. The pursuit of research-informed practice is a noble one, but in our search for 'what works' we may have created as many problems as we have solutions for the teaching profession. In this chapter, I approach these issues from a teacher-centred perspective, using my experience as a research lead to offer potential solutions to barriers to research informed practice.

BARRIERS TO RESEARCH-INFORMED TEACHING AND POTENTIAL SOLUTIONS

I have been fortunate enough to work with teachers in my roles as middle and senior leader and research lead and through my engagement with teachers at conferences. Through my own experience, the literature on the subject, and questions raised by teachers, I believe that some of the key barriers to educational leadership of research-engaged practice are:

1. Fear of failure
2. Belief that engagement with educational research is not part of a teacher's role
3. Perceived inability to engage with academic literature
4. Lack of time
5. Lack of motivation

Of course, there may be other issues that lead to a lack of support for research-informed practice, but this chapter can be viewed as a useful starting point for discussion within schools.

FEAR OF FAILURE

When we are asking teachers to engage with educational research, we must be aware that in many ways we are asking them to go against the grain of the current educational climate. We should not underestimate the impact that repeated policy changes have had in transforming the role of the teacher into one that follows through educational policy without clear opportunities to critique or shape the landscape. This culture of compliance will impact a teacher's willingness to stand back, look at their practice and question what they are doing – especially when senior leadership are watching. This can impact engagement with research in two ways: either the engagement will be surface level as teachers are unwilling to fully commit to an initiative in case it fails; or confirmation bias will yield overwhelmingly positive results because teachers have an underlying need to demonstrate success as a result of the high accountability culture. Asking a teacher to adapt their teaching is not as simple as asking teachers to change 'the way they do things' from one day to the next. For teachers, personal and professional identities are interlinked (Day et al., 2005) and so engagement with research calls for teachers to reflect on who they are in the classroom (Eraut, 1994). Subsequently, short-term action research projects will not always be enough for teachers to reflect on these bigger issues.

This happened when a cohort of teachers I've worked with undertook their first round of action research projects. Teachers adapted their teaching to include strategies that seemed applicable to our context within the educational research. This was in many ways a valuable experience, but the reflections of teachers focused overwhelming on what had worked, with no real acknowledgement of limitations or lack of success. As the member of the senior leadership team responsible for the project, I made a greater emphasis during the next round of projects on the importance of honest reflection and evaluation. If anything, the ways in which initiatives fail have equal value to the ways in which they succeed. Indeed, there are so many variables within a single classroom that we cannot ultimately determine whether something is or is not entirely effective. Perhaps this is best left to larger control trials such as those conducted by the Education Endowment Foundation. Instead, classroom enquiry can be a journey of self-exploration and an authentic reflection of our own practice. If this is something that you engage with as a teacher or school leader, then the emphasis of the process should be on reflection, rather than success. Especially when linked to performance management, you must have a clear policy that outlines that evaluation of both successes and failures is essential.

'THAT'S NOT MY JOB'

It is very tempting, when a colleague says that engaging with research is not part of teaching, to simply reply, 'Yes it is.' Kindness and open dialogue are key. Maybe they have a point? If you are closed to the idea of debate on the issue, perhaps you have an agenda contrary to genuine enquiry? The relationship between leadership and teachers is magnified with a shared focus through educational research, and lack of buy-in from teachers may be an indication of wider systemic issues of trust in a school's or MAT's leadership or values.

If there are individuals who still feel that research engagement is not part of their role, educational leaders may find themselves in a catch-22. The level of understanding a person has and the extent to which learning is internalized is limited to the extent to which an individual values the knowledge that is being transmitted. Pragmatically, one solution would be to demonstrate the presence of the need for research-informed practice in the *Teachers' Standards*[1] and if appropriate through performance management targets. I cannot stress enough that this should be a last resort to be reserved for teachers who actively resist any form of engagement with research that has been used to develop school policies. School leaders have a responsibility to ensure that all teachers feel included and actively involved in the school's ethos and culture. When the motivations behind a project are centred around improving the quality of education for children, there are very few staff who will not be willing to work together.

ABILITY TO ENGAGE WITH THE EDUCATIONAL LITERATURE

One of the key principles of effective engagement with educational research is the ability of 'experts' to share knowledge. Disseminating research must be done with a focus on relevance for teachers. This is not easy, as the theoretical and the philosophical and the empirical and the tacit must be consolidated into a codified and practical message for teachers to use as part of their practice. Even with the efforts of organisations such as the NFER and BERA, most of the research surrounding education is written for an academic audience. There are colleagues who have returned to university at some point in their career to undertake an MA in education or their subject or specialism, but for many their teacher training has been the last time that they engaged with academic literature. It is thus not condescending to support teachers to rediscover how to critique an argument or find useful books and journals online. If we are charging teachers with research engagement, then it is essential to have a clear guidance handbook and suitable CPD in this area. This could be an important aspect of the research lead's role

---

1. TS 2d: demonstrate knowledge and understanding of how pupils learn and how this impacts on teaching
    TS 4d: reflect systematically on the effectiveness of lessons and approaches to teaching
    TS 8b: develop effective profession relationships with colleagues, knowing how and when to draw on advice and specialist support
    TS 8d: take responsibility for improving teaching through appropriate professional development, responding to advice and feedback from colleagues

(discussed later in this chapter) or you are very welcome to use and adapt one I have created.

LACK OF TIME

The fact that many teachers feel overworked or under considerable pressure to perform should not be a surprise. Within the UK setting, teachers are under large amounts of pressure as a result of myriad factors such as the pressure of accountability, unrealistic marking polices and lesson preparation. 57% of teachers disagreed with the statement that their stress levels were acceptable, with 82% of teachers and 32% of senior leaders citing workload as the reason for their stress (Teacher Tapp, 2019). As it happens, there are organizations that now break down educational research into manageable reads of no more than two or three pages, whilst still ensuring the essential essence of academic rigour. The Chartered College of Teaching's journal *Impact* is fast becoming seminal to research engagement for the busy teacher. As a middle leader, I allocate time for teachers to read articles published by the Historical Association or Chartered College, which are then debated in our meetings. Not only does this deal with the issue of time management, but it also supports the message that this is a worthwhile undertaking linked to our curriculum intent and implementation.

THE PROBLEM WITH THE INDIVIDUAL

As a research lead for a small multi-academy trust, I was often faced with 'imposter syndrome' in my role. When a teacher had an issue in their classroom, I was delighted when they approached me for a solution in the literature. This delight was balanced with a sense of fear that I would not automatically know what to advise and not necessarily know a lot about the topic. This is the issue with the research lead – the double-edged sword that both creates a level of importance of and platform for engagement with educational research and misleads teachers into thinking that the research lead must have the answers. There is a history of focusing on influential individuals in education, from Thody's 'gurus' (1997) to Decroly and his 'disciples' (Van Gorp, 2006). Giving excessive influence to individuals, both within a school and beyond, undermines the purpose of research engagement. Associating ideas or principles of teaching with individuals means that there is a danger that teachers will accept or reject ideas based on their personal feelings towards school leaders or personalities rather than critically evaluating the ideas themselves. The goal of research engagement should be to empower teachers in developing their own classroom practice for the benefit of their students. Research engagement must be valued by the teaching profession as a personal journey and process of finding new knowledge rather than a system where we follow the advice of educational gurus.

The general consensus regarding the role of the research lead is supporting teachers engaging with educational research, guiding them in resourcing information that can help them find their own solutions to their areas of inquiry. Another interesting and more difficult aspect of the role is to consider the way in which research engagement highlights questions surrounding power. This means calling out senior leaders who start using 'the research suggests' when introducing new school policies when no real academic engagement has taken place. As part of their role, research leads and school leaders aim to remove barriers to research engagement. Part of this process is complexity reduction: linking actions to consequences in a streamlined way (Biesta, 2010). This can lead to deskilling the very professionals that research engagement should be empowering. I have found myself in a position where I have had to tell school leaders that I do not think their course of action is a true representation of the literature, or that it might not be a good idea to change an entire school policy based on one piece of data. Whilst this is not easy, is it is essential for research leads to do just that to avoid the totalitarianism Biesta warns us against (2010).

CONCLUSION – BE SELF-AWARE

As outlined in this chapter, teachers are under a great deal of pressure to perform well and have acclimatised to a culture that implements changes *to* teachers rather than *with* them. Listening to teachers' concerns about engaging with research should therefore be at the heart of decision making for school leaders and policy makers. Overall, my key guidance is that school leaders and research leads need to be aware of their own biases and limitations in knowledge. Teachers' various reservations about engaging with educational research all need to be acknowledged as legitimate and addressed. These views must be factored into any further steps towards developing research cultures in schools.

TOP TIPS

- Listen to teachers' concerns about engaging with research-informed practice. This should be part of the dialogue surrounding research-informed practice in schools.
- It is unreasonable to expect busy teachers to engage with research unless there are resources in place to support, such as time and easily accessible resources.
- School leaders must be aware of their own biases and limitations. Research is a positive force for teacher autonomy and school leaders must be open to challenges to the current status quo that may arise from this work.

REFERENCES

Biesta, G. (2010) 'Why "what works" still won't work: from evidence-based education to value-based education', *Studies in Philosophy and Education* 29 (5) pp. 491–503.

Brown, C., Zhang, D., Xu, N. and Corbett, S. (2018) 'Exploring the impact of social relationships on teachers' use of research: a regression analysis of 389 teachers in England', *International Journal of Educational Research* 89 (1) pp. 36–46.

Cain, T., Brindley, S., Brown, C., Jones, G. and Riga, F. (2019) 'Bounded decision-making, teachers' reflection and organisational learning: how research can inform teachers and teaching', *British Educational Research Journal* 45 (5) pp. 1072–1087.

Day, C., Kington, A., Stobart, G. and Sammons, P. (2005). 'The personal and professional selves of teachers: stable and unstable identities', *British Educational Research Journal* 32 (4) pp. 601–616.

Eraut, M. (1994) *Developing professional knowledge and competence.* Abingdon: Routledge.

Teacher Tapp (2019) 'Why are teachers walking out? The leading causes of teacher burnout', *Teacher Tapp* [Blog]. Retrieved from www.bit.ly/36UfQTZ [Accessed 19 August 2019].

Thody, A. (1997) 'Lies, damned lives and storytelling: an exploration of the contribution of principals' anecdotes to research, teaching and learning about the management of schools and colleges', *Educational Management Administration* 25 (3) pp. 325–338.

Van Gorp, A. (2006) 'Ovide Decroly, a hero of education: some reflections on the effects of educational hero worship' in Smeyers, P. and Depaepe, M. (eds) *Educational research: why 'what works' doesn't work*. Dordrecht: Springer, pp. 37–49.

KNOWLEDGE BROKERING

GARY JONES *(@DrGaryJones)*

Dr Gary Jones is the author of *Evidence-Based School Leadership and Management: A Practical Guide.* Prior to his recent work – in blogging, speaking and writing about evidence-based practice – Gary worked in the further education sector and has over 30 years of experience in education as a teacher and senior leader. Gary is currently engaged by the University of Portsmouth as a researcher on project looking at area-based reform and increasing social mobility.

INTRODUCTION

In this chapter I intend to describe my experiences as a blogger and how I first came to be writing about evidence-based practice. I'll then go onto explore a number of key themes around knowledge brokering – such as sourcing and sharing research evidence, stimulating discussion, and supporting individuals interested in making use of research. I'll then go on to explore how blogging and knowledge brokering play a sustaining role for the individual blogger. Finally, I'll reflect on any impact and success that I may have had in my role as a knowledge broker.

PERSONAL JOURNEY

I stated blogging about education in the spring of 2014 as a result of a 'professional disappointment' – which involved not being appointed to a senior position and ultimately to a change in employment status. As such, blogging was designed to provide an outlet for my interest in educational leadership and management as I tried to find a new role. Initially the blog was influenced by my 30 years of experience of working in further education, where I had seen at first hand both the negative consequences of the latest educational fads being adopted and 'teacher cultures' where 'professional interests' were prioritised over the interests of pupils, parents and other stakeholders.

However, three quite separate events then went to influence the contents of my blog posts. First, in the summer of 2014 I came across an article by Adrian Furnham in *The Sunday Times* which introduced me to work of Rob Briner, Eric Barends and Denise Rousseau on evidence-based management (Barends et al., 2014). Second, in September 2014 I attended the researchED national conference, which got me thinking about evidence-based school leadership as the vast majority of the sessions at the event had a focus on teaching and learning and little attention seemed to be being paid to the role of research and other sources of evidence in the decision making of senior leaders in schools. Third, in December 2014 I attended a researchED one-day event intended to support school research champions. At this session, it quickly became apparent that there appeared to be a lack of awareness, particularly among school research leaders, of the work being done on evidence-based practice outside of the educational sphere. Indeed, many of the presenters thought they were 'designing the plane whilst flying it' – whereas in fact they were merely re-inventing the wheel.

KEY THEMES

As a result of all this, I've ended up writing around 250 blog posts – see www.garyrjones.com/blog and my book, *Evidence-Based School Leadership and Management: A Practical Guide* (Jones, 2018) – on a range of matters relating to evidence-based or evidence-informed practice. Reflecting now on this experience as an edublogger and de facto knowledge broker and mobiliser, the following themes for discussion appear relevant: the knowledge broker as stimulator; the knowledge broker as supporter; the knowledge broker as 'sourcer' and sharer; and knowledge brokering as sustenance.

The knowledge broker as stimulator

For me, one role of the knowledge broker is to act as a stimulator, someone who is trying to provoke or stir up a discussion of some of the issues at hand. That is not to say that the attempt to provoke and stimulate discussion is designed to be deliberately mischievous; rather, what I'm trying to do is get readers to maybe pause for a moment and just challenge some of their assumptions. For example, currently there is a lot of time and effort going into trying to get teachers to make greater use of research. However, at the moment there appears to be very little (if any) evidence that research use by teachers has any positive impact on the outcomes of pupils. I have considered the research literacy – or rather lack of it – of teachers and how we need to give thought to how these issues can be addressed. Moreover, I've also written about ethics and the research- and evidence-informed school and whether there needs to be greater awareness of ethical issues when schools seek to be research informed. Furthermore, it has to be said that if you are going to try to stimulate debate, you will have to be able to 'defend' a position you have taken. For example, I recently argued that Professor John Hattie's claim that an effect size of 0.4SD is representative of year's worth of progress (Hattie, 2015) is an edu-myth. This led to my being asked to take part in a podcast with Professor Hattie, which, at the time of writing, has yet to take place.

The knowledge broker as supporter

The knowledge broker is a supporter of individuals who are undertaking the hard work of being school research leads within schools. Certainly, in early 2015, I felt that I wanted to support colleagues who were engaged in this task and who didn't necessarily have the time to access and make sense of some of the resources already available. As a consequence, I wrote a series of blog posts which focused on how school research leads could help colleagues develop well-formulated and answerable questions by using techniques and approaches which have been developed in both medicine and social science. This was followed by a series of posts which looked into how school research leads can go about creating journal clubs within their schools.

This support element of knowledge broking should not be seen as one directional, however, with me, the educational blogger, simply supporting others. I have received extensive support and encouragement from a range of individuals – academics, teachers, school leaders and 'movers and shakers' – who I have often contacted for advice or insight. For example, if I've ended up writing about something which I've not been quite sure about, I've often tried to contact someone who might actually know something about the subject and ask them for their views. In addition, I've been fortunate enough to attend a large number of conferences, allowing me to actually meet a range of people, put faces to names and develop a support network which is not entirely reliant on electronic communication and social media.

The knowledge broker as sourcer and sharer

One element of knowledge brokering and mobilisation is the process of sourcing the 'knowledge' that you want to share. Now to some extent, this process of sourcing and sharing knowledge has been both structured and random. As my writing began to focus on evidence-based practice and the school research lead, I ended up working through the process of what it takes to an be an evidence-based practitioner, so I would look for resources that explored these elements. These sources might be websites which had resources on evidence-based practice in medicine and healthcare. Alternatively, I might look at generic textbooks which looked at how to go about conducting research within the context of schools. Or I might look at journal articles which had a focus on research and evidence-informed practice within schools. And of course, I kept a constant lookout for resources produced by the Education Endowment Foundation.

On the other hand, sometimes I would end up writing a range of posts which were the product of a conversation on Twitter. For example, as a result of one such Twitter conversation I've written a number of posts on the work of Professor Tone Kvernbekk (Kvernbekk, 2016) on the role of research evidence in evidence-based practice. This subsequently led to a number of blog posts on the work of Professor Nancy Cartwright (Cartwright and Hardie, 2012) on randomised controlled trials and systematic reviews and their limitations for identifying what will work in your setting. Alternatively, posts might be the product of coming across an article in *Tes* or *Schools Week* and subsequently seeking to look at the evidence behind the headlines. But sometimes, posts might be the product of a bit of a 'lucky dip', where I put search terms into Google or Google Scholar and then hope to find something interesting and useful to write about.

Knowledge brokering as sustenance

If I am to be honest, I have to admit that there has been a selfish or egotistical element to my knowledge brokering. In large part I started edublogging because I was 'professionally lost'. I no longer had my leading position within an organisation to provide a sense of purpose for my work. Indeed, although I had effectively decided to retire early, I still felt too young to retire from the fray. As such, I used my blogging as a way of creating a new, though unpaid, role for myself. Blogging and the associated self-promotion of my work gave me a reference point for my working day. I would either be writing a blog, reading about evidence-based practice or searching the internet for resources – plus there was quite a bit of Twitter and social media. Indeed, I was fortunate enough early on in my blogging to get a bit of support from a range of individuals on Twitter – people who appeared to like what I had to say and felt that it was useful for school research leads or individuals who wished to become school research leads. As such, there is little doubt that blogging was an important part in sustaining my own personal sense of value and worth. Although in this context my blogging was focused on sharing, supporting and stimulating, the primary beneficiary of engaging in the blogging and knowledge brokering was me. Indeed, I think anyone who is engaged in knowledge brokering, especially if they are blogging, needs to spend some time reflecting on their motivation for doing the work. It also makes sense for the readers of the blog to spend some time thinking about why the blogger has written the particular post. Sometimes it might be relatively transparent from the blog itself, but in all likelihood, there is a hidden story behind the post.

IMPACT AND SUCCESS

For the independent knowledge broker, reflecting on your impact and successes is quite challenging. In terms of impact, you just don't know to any real extent who has read your blog and whether anyone, as a result of having read it, has done anything worthwhile. You end up relying on some pretty imprecise measures of success such as how many unique visitors, visits or page views you have for your posts. You might use the number of retweets or likes that you get on Twitter to help you get some sense of impact. Or you might have people email you directly asking for further guidance. Alternatively, you might use the number of invitations you get to speak at educational conferences hosted by schools and other organisations as some kind of indicator of whether your work is having any kind of impact.

As for successes, in my own terms the work I've undertaken could be judged as some form of success. I written guest blog posts for the Teacher Development Trust, the British Educational Research Association and the Centre for Evaluation and Monitoring. I've met individuals who have said I have influenced their work in schools. Indeed, someone even mentioned to me that a session I had facilitated on how to formulate questions had ultimately resulted in them leading an Education Endowment Foundation national trial. I've spoken at national and international conferences organised by, for example, the Chartered College of Teaching and the World Association of Lesson Studies. Nevertheless, to go back to why I first started edublogging and knowledge brokering, it has fulfilled its main objective: it helped me manage the period of time between full-time employment and retirement and has allowed me to maintain a sense of purpose and usefulness. As for whether it has actually been useful: well, that is for others to judge.

TOP TIPS

- Don't be frightened to contact other people interested in research use in schools – be they academics, practitioners or other bloggers. My experience has been that people are more than willing to answer emails, provide assistance and share resources. Occasionally you might get an 'abrupt' response, but in general it's the exception rather than the norm.

- It's worth have a looking at work being done in other related fields – such as improvement science and implementation science. In addition, my own experience suggests there's a whole range of resources produced in areas such as evidence-based medicine and evidence-based healthcare. These have the potential to help teachers and school leaders become more effective evidence-informed practitioners.

- This work is never done and there are always new things to learn and think about. As a knowledge broker or mobiliser – or whatever term you want to use – there's always new knowledge to mobilise and news ways to mobilise that knowledge.

REFERENCES

Barends, E., Rousseau, D. M. and Briner, R. B. (2014) *Evidence-based management : the basic principles.* Retrieved from: www.bit.ly/2On8bqa [Accessed 17 November 2020].

Cartwright, N. and Hardie, J. (2012) *Evidence-based policy: a practical guide to doing it better.* Oxford: Oxford University Press.

Hattie, J. (2015) *What doesn't work in education: the politics of distraction.* London: Pearson.

Jones, G. (2018) *Evidence-based school leadership and management: a practical guide.* London: SAGE Publishing.

Kvernbekk, T. (2016) *Evidence-based practice in education: functions of evidence and causal presuppositions.* London: Routledge.

WRITING – MY JOURNEY FROM TEACHER TO PROFESSOR

DOMINIC WYSE *(@Dominic_Wyse)*

Dominic Wyse is Professor of Early Childhood and Primary Education at the UCL Institute of Education. He is President of the British Educational Research Association, and the Founding Director of the Helen Hamlyn Centre for Pedagogy (0–11 years). Close-to-practice research has been a significant element of his work. Dominic has been researching curriculum and pedagogy for more than two decades.

The issues that connect teaching, learning and research have been important to me for at least 30 years. My understanding has grown and changed in line with my experience, which began with primary teaching and continues with university research. As a result, this chapter uses moments in my career to explore a few key points about how evidence can inform practice.

ROLES AND EXPERIENCE

My engagement with the issues that link education practice with research began in 1989 when I was a PGCE student at Goldsmiths, University of London. I became particularly interested in the teaching of writing, selecting the topic for one of the long assignments for my course. Subsequently my first teaching job was in a primary school in Somers Town in London (not far from Euston railway station). I was confident and excited about the prospect of the first 'proper' job, and in particular keen to put into practice my interest in the teaching of writing.

Six months into my first job, I could see in the children's faces that they really weren't enjoying writing. As a probationary teacher in the Inner London Education Authority (ILEA), I received half a day per week of professional development at a local teachers' centre. One of the advisory teachers recommended Donald Graves's book *Writing: Teachers and Children at Work* (Graves, 1983), and the 'process approach' to writing as it became known. That recommendation changed my professional life. It was the beginning of my journey from teacher to professor and president of the British Educational Research Association (BERA). The recommendation also had a powerful positive affect on the children in my class.

My second job as a teacher was in Bradford. Some years into the job, I enrolled to study for an MPhil part time at Leeds Metropolitan University (now Leeds Beckett University). The topic of my research was the teaching of writing. This close-to-practice research (Wyse et al., 2018) looked in depth at the pedagogy for teaching writing of a small number of teachers in my school. One of the many things I learned by undertaking the MPhil was the importance of sufficient knowledge of research methods and methodology. It is only with some understanding of methodology that we are able to make selections of research-informed ideas most likely to positively impact on practice. Teachers can acquire this knowledge from further study, but also by collaborating with more experienced researchers.

During the MPhil, Donald Graves's work reappeared, but now I became aware of criticisms. The criticisms were not of the impact of Graves's ideas – he was described as 'one of the most seductive writers in the history of writing pedagogy' (Czerniewska, 1992, p. 85) – but were about the research methods that Graves had used to develop his approach to teaching writing. Graves's career had begun as a teacher, then headteacher, then teacher trainer, and I would describe his research on writing as classic 'practitioner enquiry', a term that became popular in the 1980s. A particularly sharp criticism alleged that Graves's approach to teaching writing was based on 'unstructured expression of personal experiences' and therefore 'does not constitute research'!

> *[Graves] uses his case study of sixteen New Hampshire children as a research base providing proof of the efficacy of this method. However, his observations from this study qualify as reportage more than research. The work of the Graves team in New Hampshire represents a demonstration of teaching ideas that work well under favourable circumstances. Because he never considers negative evidence for the hypothesis he is testing, his work does not constitute research. (Smagorinsky, 1987, p. 331)*

The idea that Graves's study does not constitute proper research is extreme. This line of criticism can be seen as related to research debates that have crudely polarised research as 'scientific' (often meaning 'experimental') versus 'qualitative', including qualitative case-study research (see Wyse et al., 2017, for a recent review of such debates). However, although Graves's ideas appeared to work and were very popular with teachers in a range of countries, and although his research could not fairly be described as 'reportage', it was nevertheless just one relatively small-scale study. One important outcome of such research is that it can stimulate larger scale research to examine the hypotheses made as a result of the qualitative research or practitioner enquiry.

IMPACT OF RESEARCH-INFORMED TEACHING

In the decades since Graves's original study, we now have the benefit of larger-scale experimental trial evidence. A recent systematic review and meta-analysis (Graham et al., 2016) found 33 experimental studies which had compared a process writing approach to a control condition ('business as usual' or a different approach to teaching writing). The meta-analysis of these studies found a statistically significant effect for the process writing approach (see table 1), with an effect size (EF) of 0.34 overall. Effect sizes go beyond simply establishing whether an approach has worked or not. They indicate how well it worked, through their measure of the extent of difference between comparison groups in experimental studies. An effect size from 0.26 to 0.44, equivalent to a range of three to six months' progress, is considered moderate (Higgins et al., 2012). Although the process writing approach was effective with both primary and secondary students, it was more effective with primary or elementary students (grades 1–5), with an effect size of 0.48, as opposed to an effect size of 0.25 for secondary students.

Interventions	Studies	Effect size	95% confidence interval	Grade levels
Process writing	33	0.34***	0.24 to 0.44	1–12
Elementary/primary	18	0.48***	0.34 to 0.65	1–5
Secondary	14	0.25***	0.12 to 0.39	6–12

Table 1: Meta-analysis of experimental studies of the process writing approach (informed by Graham et al., 2016, p. 211)[1]

As a result of adopting some of Graves's ideas, the motivation for writing of the children in my class in Somers Town became transformed. Instead of 'Oh no, not writing again,' children began to say, 'When can we do writing workshop again?' Their creativity and confidence began to shine through (for a fuller account see Wyse, 1998).

Many years later, starting in 2014, I began an ambitious new study, this time researching writing for children and adults across the life course. The study was to last four years and involved not only newly funded empirical studies (including a three-year longitudinal study of creativity in writing) but also new investigations into philosophies of writing, histories of writing, and the world of both novices and some of the world's most eminent writers. The approach was deliberately multi-disciplinary. One endpoint of the study was my book *How Writing Works: From the Invention of the Alphabet to the Rise of Social Media* (Wyse, 2017). But in another way this work and the book was only a beginning.

---

1. 'Note. All average-weighted effect sizes are for writing quality except effects for Writing about Content Material (content learning measured) and Writing about Material Read (reading comprehension measured) … *** p < .001' (Graham et al., 2016, p. 211).

Building on the *How Writing Works* study, a new close-to-practice research project was started. This involved a small number of teachers interested in changing how writing was taught in their classes and schools. The project included professional development opportunities for the teachers, combined with a form of design research. For the research, the teachers were presented with seven principles that I derived from my *How Writing Works* project (and Graham et al., 2016):

1. Increase the amount of time spent writing.
2. Create a supportive writing environment in the classroom.
3. Develop pupils' skills, strategies and knowledge.
4. Teach pupils about 'self-regulation'.
5. Use assessment for learning techniques.
6. Teach keyboard use as well as handwriting.
7. Teach writing across the curriculum.

The teachers had to plan a new approach to teaching writing which they would trial, work with the researcher to document, then report back on. The only requirement was that the approach be rooted in at least some of the seven principles. At the end of the year, it was striking to see not only the teachers' reports of the positive impacts on the children in their classes but also how the new approaches to pedagogy had permanently changed their practice and their confidence as teachers more generally.

An important element of the work was that the research evidence was presented in a form that was amenable to use in practice; it was non-prescriptive; it encouraged the teachers to be creative with their practice but also to be accountable to the research evidence in the principles and to their professional contexts.

SYSTEMS TO SUPPORT RESEARCH-INFORMED TEACHING

There are many, many challenges to achieving research-informed teaching that is likely to have a beneficial effect on children's learning, but one I want to focus on in the limited words available in this chapter: the selection of research. There are currently many voices implying that their approach to evidence-informed practice is best. For example, there are people (and sometimes their organisations) with high social media profiles; there are views from government; university researchers are seeking engagement and impact; teacher organisations such as unions are involved; and so on. How should a teacher or an institution choose which research to pay attention to? In my view, here are the points to take account of when selecting evidence to inform practice:

- Try to select summaries of evidence that rigorously combine multiple studies rather than rely unduly on single studies.
- Prioritise work from researchers and research teams who not only understand research but who have the closest and most in-depth understanding of the nature of educational practice.
- Recognise that for most topics there are many evidence sources, often accumulated over decades, that need to be taken account of.
- Where possible, access summaries of evidence from a range of disciplines, not least education as an academic discipline.
- Understand that different research questions require answers from different research designs.
- Recognise that for some topics or issues there simply isn't sufficient research to guide practice, in which case professionals' own everyday evidence is doubly important.

This book is all about the processes by which education practitioners can access and use the best evidence to inform their educational practice. In fact, the topic of how research can inform practice has itself been researched. This research suggests that the likelihood of evidence being used by professionals to make decisions is increased if the intervention explicitly addresses the capability, motivation and opportunity of the professionals to use the new evidence-informed practice.

Interventions that support the communication of and access to research evidence were only effective to increase evidence use if the intervention design simultaneously tried to enhance decision-makers' opportunity and motivation to use evidence. It is therefore advisable that future research and practice focus on how to design and tailor interventions that better feature these CMO [capability, motivation and opportunity] configurations. In this, social science offers a great deal of knowledge that can be drawn upon. (Langer et al., 2016, p. 9)

The British Educational Research Association (BERA),was formed in the 1970s because of a concern with how education practice and education research might be represented in universities, including as part of teacher training, teacher education and professional development. Lawrence Stenhouse, one of the first presidents of BERA, commented on the early development of education departments in universities in the 1970s:

The teaching of education as an undifferentiated field has been largely supplanted by the teaching of constituent disciplines. Philosophy, psychology and sociology are virtually everywhere represented … This change in curriculum has increased the rigour and the intellectual tone of education courses. It has done little for their relevance to the problem of improving the practice of teaching. (Stenhouse, 1975, p. vii)

Understanding the processes by which evidence can influence practice is important, but this knowledge of processes is worthless without concurrent attention to, and knowledge about, the substantive research related to a given topic, whether that is the teaching of writing, mental health and wellbeing, music, creativity, or any topic that practitioners and researchers decide is in need of research. When education researchers work closely with practitioners, and education practice is in sync with education research, the capacity to develop new understandings is limitless.

TOP TIPS

- Take an active interest in how research can inform practice – develop your critical understanding of research claims.
- Work with a researcher to examine a topic of mutual interest.
- Carry out a piece of research to evaluate practice in your classroom or setting/school.

REFERENCES

Czerniewska, P. (1992) *Learning about writing.* Oxford: Blackwell.

Graham, S., Harris, K. and Chambers, A. (2016) 'Evidence-based practice and writing instruction: a review of reviews', in MacArthur, C. A., Graham, S. and Fitzgerald, J. (eds) *Handbook of writing research.* 2nd edn. New York, NY: Guilford Press, pp. 211–227.

Graves, D. H. (1983) *Writing: teachers and children at work.* Portsmouth, NH: Heinemann.

Higgins, S., Kokotsaki, D. and Coe, R. (2012) *The teaching and learning toolkit: technical appendices.* London: Education Endowment Foundation and The Sutton Trust.

Langer, L., Tripney, J. and Gough, D. (2016) *The science of using science: researching the use of research evidence in decision-making.* London: UCL Institute of Education Press.

Smagorinsky, P. (1987) 'Graves revisited: a look at the methods and conclusions of the New Hampshire study', *Written Communication* 4 (4) pp. 331–342.

Stenhouse, L. (1975) *An introduction to curriculum research and development.* London: Heinemann.

Wyse, D. (1998) *Primary writing.* Buckingham: Open University Press.

Wyse, D. (2017) *How writing works: from the birth of the alphabet to the rise of social media.* Cambridge: Cambridge University Press.

Wyse, D., Brown, C., Oliver, S. and Pobleté, X. (2018) *The BERA close-to-practice research project: research report.* London: British Educational Research Association. Retrieved from www.bit.ly/2P1ivVk [Accessed 12 January 2020].

Wyse, D., Smith, E., Selwyn, N. and Suter, L. (2017) 'Editors' introduction' in Wyse, D., Smith, E., Selwyn, N. and Suter, L. (eds) *The SAGE international handbook of educational research.* London: SAGE, pp. 1–35.

RESEARCH-INFORMED TEACHING
AND TEACHER PROFESSIONAL STATUS

CAT SCUTT *(@CatScutt)*

Cat is Director of Education and Research at the Chartered College of
Teaching, the professional body for the teaching profession. She leads
on their work around teacher development and research engagement,
including their publications and Chartered Teacher programme.

INTRODUCTION

Engaging with research and evidence has a whole host of short- and long-
term benefits for teachers and school leaders, many of which are explored
in other chapters in this book. This includes, critically, the positive impact
we would ultimately expect to see on student outcomes (Brown, 2017).

But in my role at the Chartered College of Teaching, I am particularly
interested in the relationship between research use and teacher confidence,
the trust and autonomy afforded to teachers, and the status of teaching
as a profession. These areas are closely linked to teacher job satisfaction,
which relates to teacher retention – and this, too, of course, ultimately
leads to more experienced and effective teachers, in turn leading to better
outcomes for children and young people (Kraft and Papay, 2014).

NOTIONS OF PROFESSIONS AND PROFESSIONALISM

It's worth starting by reflecting on what we mean by teaching as a
'profession', and how the idea of being research-informed links to this.

Whilst definitions of a profession are contested, Gomendio (2017) and others note a number of features that distinguish a profession from a semi-profession, including:

- A high level of public trust and confidence
- An extended training period
- A collective body of knowledge and expertise, built on a theoretical base, that is shared by members of the profession
- High levels of professional autonomy, with limited amounts of supervision

It is easy to see how these can be linked to the idea of a profession being research-informed: a strong, shared knowledge base seems dependent on teachers having an understanding of the best available research evidence, whilst public trust and high levels of autonomy seem more likely where teachers' expertise and up-to-date knowledge of the best-evidenced approaches are acknowledged.

Clearly, strides have been made towards teaching being a research-informed profession over the past few years; much has changed since Ben Goldacre's plea for evidence to be built into education (Goldacre, 2013). Movements such as ResearchED and organisations such as the Education Endowment Foundation and the Chartered College of Teaching have gained momentum, with ever-greater numbers of teachers and school leaders recognising the impact that engaging with research can have. But although the progress to date is encouraging, there is still much to do (Walker et al., 2019). The level of research-engagement varies substantially across the system (Coldwell et al., 2017), both between and within schools. So how can we best continue the journey?

UNDERSTANDING EVIDENCE-INFORMED PRACTICE

Any discussion about research and evidence use would be incomplete without some consideration of terminology. This book adopts the term 'research-informed', whilst a range of other terms are used elsewhere, often largely interchangeably – including 'evidence-based', 'research-engaged,' and even 'evidence-enriched' (Stoll, 2017). Is this just a question of semantics, or is there important debate to be had? Arguments for one term over another tend to centre on two questions: firstly, what is meant by 'research' or 'evidence'; and secondly, the nature of how this is used in teaching practice. Both of these are worth reflecting on briefly, drawing on ideas from discussions with a range of teachers.

Whilst there is undoubtedly huge crossover between the terms 'research' and 'evidence', particularly in regard to published research evidence, some have noted that the former implies not just making use of research conducted elsewhere, but also conducting one's own research. Whilst the value of engaging with research is increasingly universally recognised, there remains debate over whether teachers should or can reasonably be expected to carry out their own research, given the time involved, as well as whether sufficiently robust impact evaluation is likely to be able to take place. The term 'evidence', meanwhile, could be argued to encompass a wider range of sources to inform decision-making, including school data or even pupils' views, in addition to academic research. This broader thinking is valued, but in some cases the term 'evidence' is also associated with a need to 'prove' oneself and overbearing approaches to monitoring and accountability.

Both the terms 'research' and 'evidence', then, have their advantages and disadvantages. But it is the question of whether we should be aiming for the profession to be research-*informed* or research-*based* that is particularly pertinent when thinking about the relationship between use of research evidence and teacher autonomy. It has been argued that the term 'evidence-based' risks suggesting that teachers should act solely on research evidence, reducing the value of teachers' professional expertise, whilst 'research-informed' more clearly recognises that research evidence will only ever be part of the picture in informing teachers' decision-making.

Gary Jones (2018) argues, however, that this position misunderstands the whole principle of evidence-based practice. Sackett et al.'s definition of evidence-based practice in medicine as 'the conscientious, explicit, and judicious use of current best evidence in making decisions about the care of individual patients … integrating individual clinical expertise with the best available external clinical evidence from systematic research' (Sackett et al., 1996, p. 71) clearly highlights that professional expertise is as much a part of evidence-based practice as the use of published research.

I would argue, then, that whilst it is perfectly reasonable to use the terms 'research-informed', 'evidence-informed', 'research-based' and 'evidence-based' largely interchangeably, it's important to recognise *why* some teachers may prefer one over the other. As such, I tend to use the term 'evidence-informed', defining such practice in education as 'the critical use of the current best available evidence from research alongside teachers' experience, expertise and professional judgement, to inform approaches to the teaching of individual students and groups of students in context' (Scutt, 2018).

CONNECTING RESEARCH AND PRACTICE

Critically, in this definition I seek to recognise the three strands of evidence-informed practice – published research, teachers' professional expertise, and the context in which they are working – and to avoid any sense that research will tell teachers what to do. Evidence will not provide a silver bullet for the many and complex problems that teachers face on a daily basis. And, as Dylan Wiliam reminds us, context is key: 'everything works somewhere and nothing works everywhere' (Wiliam, 2015).

However, by combining their professional expertise and experience with the best available evidence, teachers can make more-informed decisions about the best approaches for their own specific context and their intended outcomes, and feel confident that they are doing so. This is not always about changing what we do: sometimes research reaffirms or adds depth to something we already know; sometimes it challenges our existing practice, helping us to spend less time on ineffective practices; and sometimes it brings new ideas to our practice.

Using research evidence in this way can also help teachers to articulate the reasons for the choices they make in the classroom. Education blogger David Didau has even gone as far as to suggest that this dialogue could form an effective part of teacher observation (Didau, 2018). Supporting teachers to engage with research and be able to explain both *what* is happening in their classrooms and *why* it is happening can thus be part of a move to provide teachers with greater professional confidence and autonomy.

BARRIERS TO TEACHING AS A RESEARCH-INFORMED PROFESSION

This is all very well in theory, but using research to inform practice is far from straightforward; approaches to supporting teachers to engage in evidence-informed practices can struggle to have any impact (Lord et al., 2017). From being motivated to make use of research, to practical issues such as having access to relevant, high-quality research and the time to engage with it, to the difficulty in changing habits and the skills required to design, implement and evaluate new research-based approaches, there are significant challenges across many of the steps involved in evidence-informed teaching.

Whilst a recent study by NFER for the Education Endowment Foundation (Walker et al., 2019) found that teachers are, on average, reasonably positive about the idea of using research, the myriad pressures and demands on teachers' time can make it hard for research engagement to be prioritised. The time required to locate, filter and read extended research reports is significant; and in some cases, of course, there simply isn't high-quality research that answers the questions teachers may have. Research expertise is necessary for teachers to be able to identify research that is both relevant to their practice and sufficiently robust to be valuable. There is therefore an increasing interest in helping teachers to develop the 'research literacy' required to critically appraise original research, consider the implications a piece of research may have and what conclusions it is reasonable to draw from its findings. And even where the implications of research are relatively clear, changing long-established habits and practices is difficult, particularly in a high-paced environment like a classroom.

A number of organisations offer useful resources to help overcome some of these barriers. The Education Endowment Foundation provide useful toolkits of research overviews as well as guidance reports to support implementation in practice and a national network of research schools offering CPD, support and regular communications to help teachers to engage with research effectively. The *Best Evidence in Brief* newsletter from the Institute for Effective Education offers fortnightly summaries of the latest research, whilst The Learning Scientists publish blogs, resources and podcasts the science of learning. ResearchED's conferences and magazines give teachers the opportunity to engage with and debate the latest research findings and practice. Membership of the Chartered College also provides access to an extensive education research database and curated research summaries, as well as a termly practitioner journal – *Impact* – and our online member platform includes original research, written and video case studies and reflections on research in use.

A CULTURE OF RESEARCH ENGAGEMENT

However, even where all of the barriers above are addressed, any move to encourage teachers to be research-informed seems destined to fail if they are not working in a school environment that is also research-informed. If a teacher understands the evidence about, for example, marking and feedback, and yet a school's policy requires extensive written marking or 'verbal feedback' stamps on all pupil work, the teacher will not feel able to work in a research-informed way, and their professional autonomy will be limited. This is likely to lead to the same sorts of frustrations experienced by teachers where the CPD they engage in does not align with school practices (Knight, 2002).

A culture of research engagement is about more than just school policies being research-informed, however. It's also about creating a culture where teachers are given time and space to collaborate around research use, and where the value of this is recognised.

And these principles extend to the system level, too (Godfrey and Brown, 2018); it is hard for schools to aim to take evidence-based decisions if these clash with what is expected in national policy or accountability systems, or simply if the system itself does not seem research-informed. System-level policies around grammar school expansion, for example, have been widely criticised for its failure to be grounded in evidence. But we also need a system where teachers have career pathways and opportunities around research use, and where there is a mutually supportive relationship between research and practice, and between researchers and practitioners.

CONCLUSION: SUPPORTIVE CULTURES

Engaging with research can play a key role not just in developing teachers' practice and improving student outcomes, but also in building teachers' confidence, job satisfaction and supporting teacher retention. However, if we want teaching to be a research-informed profession, we need to ensure teachers are working in an environment where this is supported. If you are a teacher interested in evaluating where you are on your journey to evidence-informed practice, or a school leader who wants to evaluate your school's level of research engagement, you might find the Chartered College of Teaching's free 'evidence-informed teaching' self-evaluation toolkits useful. These were developed by researchers from Durham University, Sheffield Hallam University and UCL Institute of Education based on their work on research engagement carried out for the Department for Education (Coldwell et al, 2017). They also include examples and recommendations for teachers and schools at every stage of research use. The Education Endowment Foundation's guide to implementation for schools (Sharples et al., 2018) also provides useful guidance on planning, developing and evaluating the roll-out of evidence-based practices across a school.

TOP TIPS

Whether you're thinking about your own practice, or that of colleagues in your school, don't forget:

- Research evidence won't tell teachers what to do, but it can help them to make informed decisions and to reflect on and articulate their practice.
- We need to break down the practical barriers to research engagement – such as a lack of time and access to research – but more importantly, we need to create motivation to engage with research by ensuring that it's seen as a worthwhile endeavour.

- If we want teachers to be research-informed, they need to be working in a school and system that is research-informed, too, so we need to think about research-informed policy as well as practice.

REFERENCES

Brown, C. (2017) 'Research learning communities: how the RLC approach enables teachers to use research to improve their practice and the benefits for students that occur as a result', *Research for All* 1 (2) pp. 387–405.

Coldwell, M., Greany, T., Higgins, S., Brown, C., Maxwell, B., Stiell, B., Stoll, L., Willis, B. and Burns, H. (2017) *Evidence-informed teaching: an evaluation of progress in England*. Department for Education. London: The Stationery Office. Retrieved from: www.bit.ly/2UDWeAl [Accessed 1 December 2019].

Didau, D. (2018) 'Should Ofsted observe lessons?', *Learning Spy* [Blog], 31 May. Retrieved from: www.bit.ly/2ulwgXF [Accessed 30 November 2019].

Godfrey, D. and Brown, C. D. (2018) 'How effective is the research and development ecosystem for England's schools?', *London Review of Education* 16 (1) pp. 136–151.

Goldacre, B. (2013) *Building evidence into education*. Department for Education. London: The Stationery Office.

Gomendio, M. (2017) *Empowering and enabling teachers to improve equity and outcomes for all*. Paris: OECD Publishing.

Jones, G. (2018) 'Evidence-based practice: what it is and what it isn't', *CEMblog*, 20 March. Retrieved from www.bit.ly/2Op8DnZ [Accessed 30 November 2019].

Knight, P. (2002) 'A systemic approach to professional development: learning as practice', *Teaching and Teacher Education* 18 (3) pp. 229–241.

Kraft, M. A. and Papay, J. P. (2014) 'Can professional environments in schools promote teacher development? Explaining heterogeneity in returns to teaching experience', *Educational Evaluation and Policy Analysis* 36 (4) pp. 476–500.

Lord, P., Rabiasz, A., Roy, P., Harland, J., Styles, B. and Fowler, K. (2017) *Evidence-based literacy support: the 'Literacy Octopus' trial*. London: Education Endowment Foundation.

Sackett, D. L., Rosenberg, W. M., Gray, J. A., Haynes, R. B. and Richardson, W. S. (1996) 'Evidence based medicine: what it is and what it isn't', *British Medical Journal* 312 (7023) pp. 71–72.

Scutt, C. (2018) 'Is engaging with and in research a worthwhile investment for teachers?' in Carden, C. (ed.) *Primary teaching*. London: Learning Matters, pp. 595–609.

Sharples, J., Albers, B., Fraser, S. and Kime, S. (2018) *Putting evidence to work: a school's guide to implementation*. London: Education Endowment Foundation.

Stoll, L. (2017) 'Five challenges in moving towards evidence-informed practice', *Impact* (interim issue). Retrieved from www.bit.ly/38GOphD [Accessed 28 November 2019].

Walker, M., Nelson, J. and Bradshaw, S. with Brown, C. (2019) *Teachers' engagement with research: what do we know? A research briefing*. London: Education Endowment Foundation.

Wiliam, D. (2015) 'The research delusion', *Tes*, 10 April. Retrieved from: www.bit.ly/2SXGeXg [Accessed 30 November 2019].

CHALLENGES AND POSSIBILITIES FOR RESEARCH-INFORMED TEACHING

JULIE NELSON (*@Nelson_Julie_A*)

Dr Julie Nelson directs a variety of research and evaluation studies on research-informed teaching and teacher continuing professional development (CPD) for the Education Endowment Foundation (EEF), the Department for Education (DfE) and the Wellcome Trust. She is co-author of a review: *Using Evidence in the Classroom: what works and why?*; was Guest Editor of a special issue of *Educational Research* on evidence-informed practice in education; and is co-author of the chapter 'Evidence use in Education' in *What Works Now?*, edited by Annette Boaz et al.

INTRODUCTION

For a number of years, I have been involved in research and practical projects to support the use of research in education. With colleagues, I have investigated what research-informed teaching means for busy school leaders and teachers. I have led evaluations that aim to explain why research-informed teaching matters; how it can help schools; and what its potential impacts are.

My work also involves gathering evidence to improve awareness of the conditions that make it easier, or more challenging, for research-informed teaching to be achieved. This work has generated messages for educational stakeholders at different levels within the education system about things that are working well, and other things that might need to change or be enhanced.

In this chapter, I share some of these insights and hope that they will prove useful for school leaders and teachers at various stages of the research-informed teaching journey.

WHAT DOES BEING RESEARCH INFORMED MEAN?

What do we mean by 'research'?

There is an ongoing debate about what constitutes *good* research, with much discussion about the robustness and value of different methodologies – for example, randomised controlled trials (RCTs), qualitative studies and mixed-methods approaches (Bredo, 2006; Nutley et al, 2013).

To my mind, the important question for school leaders and teachers to ask is 'What question am I trying to answer?' or 'What challenge am I trying to address?' If you want to know which teaching pedagogies are most effective in improving pupil outcomes, then syntheses of RCT evidence, such as those summarised in the EEF's *Toolkit* (2018) are likely to be best. However, if you want to understand views on an issue, or to understand how a teaching approach is received, then other types of research (such as longitudinal surveys, qualitative or mixed-methods approaches) may be more appropriate. It is important to understand the benefits and limitations of different types of research when you make decisions about what to read and discuss and whether to implement the learning.

Most proponents of research-informed teaching encourage teachers to engage with academic or professional research and this is important. However, there is also a place for teacher-led enquiry as a means of understanding day-to-day classroom practice and as a support for professional reflection and discussion (Bryk et al., 2011; Stoll, 2015). As with any small-scale endeavour (whether conducted by an academic or a teacher), enquiry findings are unlikely to be suitable for replication (copying elsewhere). This is because, in most cases, they will not have been subjected to wider-scale testing, and we cannot know that what seems effective in one place will work in another. One exception is the Education Development Trust's Test and Learn programme (Churches et al., 2019), which enables teachers to conduct mini-RCT projects, with a view to replication.

What do we mean by 'informed'?

Research is just one of many sources that teachers can use to aid decision making and practices. Practice-based sources (for example, teacher assessments and professional judgement) are equally important. Research-informed practice should not be about teachers *basing* their practice on research without critique. It should be about 'blending' professional judgement with new knowledge and making sensible adaptations, so that the research 'fits' the local school or classroom context.

I would define a research-informed teacher to be a reflective practitioner with a desire to extend their professional knowledge by drawing on research sources and/or support from beyond their immediate experience or teacher networks. They actively critique these sources while applying their professional expertise. They are innovative and experimental professionals and have the motivation, skills and opportunities to implement research findings in their practice. You may accept or disagree with this, or find that some aspects, but not all, ring true for you.

NFER has conducted recent surveys of teachers in England to explore levels of research engagement. We found that, although teachers generally had positive views about research evidence, research had a relatively small impact on their decision making or practice. This suggests that there is still work to do to develop the 'implementation' aspect of research-informed teaching outlined in box 1 (Nelson et al., 2017; Walker et al., 2019).

WHY DOES IT MATTER? WHAT IS THE POTENTIAL IMPACT?

Although a causal link has not yet been established between research-informed teaching and improved pupil outcomes, there is growing evidence that it can aid school improvement (Mincu, 2013; Cordingley et al., 2015; Greany, 2015). A number of studies have shown benefits for schools that engage with research. These are outlined below and in figure 1.

1. Teacher quality

There is evidence that research-informed teaching and research-informed CPD can both support teacher quality. In turn, many studies have shown that improving teacher quality is the most direct route to improving pupil, and school, outcomes.

2. Innovation and experimentation

Brown et al. (2016) showed that having a high level of trust between senior leaders and teachers was a strong predictor of schools having a culture of research use. High levels of trust ensure that teachers feel confident about questioning their practice and/or taking informed risks to try out new things in a supported environment. Research-informed teachers can bring innovation and experimentation to their schools.

3. Identification of 'promising approaches'

Finally, because research-informed teachers know how to find evidence of promising approaches, they are able to make recommendations about research-informed changes that could be made in their schools. This is most effective in schools that actively support staff to innovate and experiment. Schools can save time and money by carefully selecting evidence-based programmes, or research-informed guidance, that fit with their priorities for school improvement.

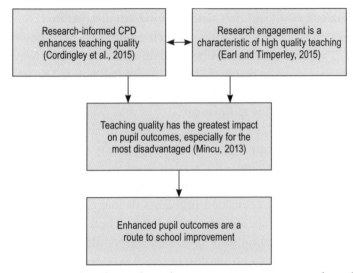

Figure 1: Research-informed teaching as a route to improved teaching quality and school improvement

WHAT PREVENTS RESEARCH-INFORMED PRACTICE, AND HOW CAN YOU OVERCOME THIS?

There are a number of challenges to research-informed practice, some of which are discussed below.

1. Educational policy and community issues

NFER and Chris Brown recently conducted a study for the EEF which considered the challenges for evidence-informed school improvement (Walker et al., 2020). Interviewees identified four external challenges which often acted as a brake on innovation or engagement with evidence-informed support:

- **The accountability system** – in particular the pressures associated with Ofsted inspections, and the need to show rapid progress. This sometimes resulted in a scattergun approach to improvement, rather than a measured and sustained one (Ehren, 2019; Greany and Earley, 2018).

- **Austerity** – meant that schools could not always afford to support their staff to engage with research evidence (Díaz-Gibson et al., 2017; Greany, 2017). When exercised well, research-informed practice can *save* resources by aiding swifter, tailored decisions, but it takes bravery on the part of senior leaders to trust that the initial investment will reap rewards.
- **Staff supply** – in particular problems of staff recruitment and retention (Hargreaves et al., 2015). Many schools suffer from diminished staffing and a high level of 'churn', which makes sustaining research-informed practice difficult.
- **Poverty** – and associated problems of low parental engagement, poor pupil behaviour and attendance. Many schools found that they were spending disproportionate amounts of time and money filling gaps left by an erosion of social services support, which left them with limited resources or energy for research engagement.

2. Supply of research evidence

In spite of recent developments which have transformed the supply of research for schools – for example, the EEF; the Chartered College of Teaching (www.chartered.college); the Research Schools Network (www. researchschool.org.uk); and researchED (www.researched.org.uk) – there is still room for improvement. More needs to be done to synthesise and simplify research studies for easy access by teachers (Gough, 2013), and to provide implementation guidelines (Sharples, 2013). The purpose of academic research is not always to write for a school audience, so 'translation' work is also important. There are a number of 'brokerage' organisations that are well placed (in principle, if not always in practice) to help with this – for example: teaching school alliances; multi-academy trusts and national leaders of education (Nutley, 2013; Sharples, 2013).

3. School climate

The challenges outlined above are, to a large extent, outside the control of schools, but there are other, within-school challenges. Our research showed that school leaders sometimes struggled with effective diagnosis of need, for example focusing on external challenges, rather than specific and precise changes that they could make in their schools. We also found that they sometimes lacked the confidence to support their colleagues to use research effectively, or had a tendency to jump to an available solution before the challenge itself had been properly defined: 'What you often see with school leaders in difficult situations is that they will try lots of different things in the hope that something works' (System leader statement, cited in Walker et al., 2020).

SO, HOW CAN YOU SUCCESSFULLY INCORPORATE RESEARCH INTO YOUR PRACTICE?

If the education system is to become more research informed, a system-wide approach is essential. Efforts are underway to improve the supply, coordination and implementation of research. But there are also things that schools can do.

Build the right school culture and climate: points for practitioners

Research-informed teaching is most likely to flourish if it is actively supported by school leaders. If you are a school leader, it is important that you present a vision, outlining why it is important. You need to back this up with practical support and resources, and then you need to lead by example, ideally modelling practice and/or providing coaching support (Brown and Zhang, 2016; Coldwell et al., 2017; Roberts, 2015).

There are some freely available resources to help you establish where you are on this journey. These include NFER's Self-Review Tool;[1] the Coalition for Evidence-based Education's *Leading Research Engagement in Education* guide;[2] and the Chartered College of Teaching's evidence-engagement self-assessment toolkits, produced by Sheffield Hallam University and colleagues.[3]

---

1.   www.bit.ly/2OtaZ50
2.   www.bit.ly/31A7pf3
3.   www.bit.ly/31mIBHa

Have a process for identifying, using and reviewing research

Figure 2 presents a fairly simple cycle. In practice, there are many points in this where efforts can fail. Much hinges on making sure that you have a systematic approach to tackling every step of the process.

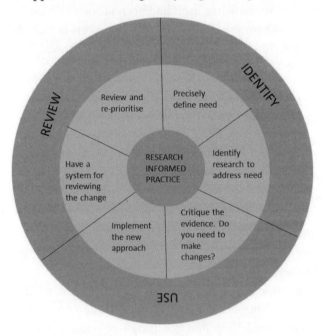

Figure 2: Identify, use, review cycle

Identification

Research must serve the needs of schools, pupils and teachers, so the obvious starting point is to precisely diagnose your need and then to look for research evidence that might offer some solutions. It is surprising how often this is not the starting point for research engagement. We know that some senior leaders find it difficult to convert their challenges into questions that can be answered by research. There are many research-to-practice intermediaries that can help you or your school to do this. One CPD provider in our recent research study explained how they had helped a school to move 'from a focus on "white working-class boys"' [achievement] to questions like "How can I help my students become more independent learners?'" (Walker et al., 2020).

Use

Before jumping to action, first critique the research by asking questions such as 'Is it robust?' or 'Was the method appropriate?' Then consider your current approaches, and decide whether these would benefit from change. Apply your professional judgement in deciding 'Would this work in my school?' or 'Do we need to adapt the approach so that it will work here?' It is important to work through these and other questions before embarking on any change.

Review

Finally, make sure you have put in place a systematic process for reviewing the implementation. This element of the process often fails, but without it, it is difficult to know whether the development was beneficial, and whether or not it needs adaptation. A respondent in our research study confirmed that, for them: 'The important bit is the trialling, testing and tweaking' (Walker et al., 2020, p. xx). Also remember that, as another of our participants commented: 'An evidence-informed approach is a long-term approach to sustained school improvement. It's not about the "shiny new thing"' (Walker et al., 2020).

CONCLUSION – THE PRIZE TO BE WON

Research-informed teaching has the power to have a transformative effect on the education system. It matters because it is a feature of high-quality teaching and can enhance teacher quality; and developing teacher quality is a well-recognised route to improving pupil, and school, outcomes. Research-informed teachers are innovative and experimental; they know where to go to find promising research evidence; and they have the motivation, skills and opportunities to implement research findings in their practice. These skills and practices should be encouraged and nurtured.

Although there are multiple challenges (at policy, community and school levels) which often hinder research-informed teaching, there is much that schools can do to overcome these and create fertile ground for it to flourish (Nelson and Campbell, 2017). Senior leaders need to be visionary and brave; but they also need to provide practical systems, structures and resources that will enable their staff to access and engage with research sources, learn to appraise and critique these, and be supported to consider whether, and how, they could be applied in practice. Systems for monitoring and reviewing the implementation of new approaches are also essential.

The prize is increased school decision-making confidence and efficiency, with less time spent trying out approaches that may, or may not, have promise; an engaged, innovative and autonomous staff body; high-quality teaching; and, ultimately, the potential for highly achieving pupils and schools.

TOP TIPS

- Diagnose your issue, and then prioritise specific research question(s). Keep these manageable. Seek research that can help you to answer them.
- Focus on what you or your school can achieve, rather than the scale of the external challenges that you face.
- Be brave – trust that improvements in teaching quality and practice, and the identification of promising approaches, will offset your initial and ongoing costs.
- Senior leaders, provide a vision for your staff, and back this up with practical systems, structures and resources to enable them to engage and apply the learning.

REFERENCES

Bredo, E. (2006) 'Philosophies of educational research' in Green, J. L., Camilli, G., Elmore, P. B. with Skukauskaitė, A. and Grace, E. (eds) *Handbook of complementary methods in education research*. Washington, DC: American Educational Research Association; Mahwah, NJ: Lawrence Erlbaum Associates, pp. 3–31.

Brown, C. and Zhang, D. (2016) 'Is engaging in evidence-informed practice in education rational? What accounts for discrepancies in teachers' attitudes towards evidence use and actual instances of evidence use in schools?', *British Education Research Journal* 42 (5) pp. 780–801.

Brown, C., Daly, A. and Liou, Y. (2016) 'Improving trust, improving schools: findings from a social network analysis of 43 primary schools in England', *Journal of Professional Capital & Community* 1 (1) pp. 69–91.

Bryk, A. S., Gomez, L. M. and Grunow, A. (2011) 'Getting ideas into action: building networked improvement communities in education', in Hallinan, M. T. (ed.) *Frontiers in sociology of education.* Dordrecht: Springer, pp. 127–162.

Churches, R., Korin, A. and Sims, K. (2019) *Test and learn: a global revolution in teacher-led research.* Reading: Education Development Trust. Retrieved from: www.bit.ly/31rqb7X [Accessed 6 December 2019].

Coldwell, M., Greany, T., Higgins, S., Brown, C., Maxwell, B., Stiell, B., Stoll, L., Willis, B. and Burns, H. (2017) *Evidence-informed teaching: an evaluation of progress in England.* Department for Education. London: The Stationery Office. Retrieved from: www.bit.ly/2UDWeAl [Accessed 4 December 2019].

Cordingley, P., Higgins, S., Greany, T., Buckler, N., Coles-Jordan, D., Crisp, B., Saunders, L. and Coe, R. (2015) *Developing great teaching: lessons from the international reviews into effective professional development* [Online]. Retrieved from: www.bit.ly/36XNsiY [Accessed 4 December 2019].

Díaz-Gibson, J., Zaragoza, M. C., Daly, A. J., Mayayo, J. L. and Romaní, J. R. (2017) 'Networked leadership in educational collaborative networks', *Educational Management Administration & Leadership* 45 (6) pp. 1040–1059.

Earl, L. and H. Timperley (2015) *Evaluative thinking for successful educational innovation.* OECD Education Working Papers, No. 122. Paris: OECD Publishing.

Education Endowment Foundation (2018) *Teaching and Learning Toolkit* [Online]. Retrieved from www.bit.ly/2RUkdZ6 [Accessed 4 December 2019].

Ehren, M. (2019) 'Accountability structures that support school self-evaluation, enquiry and learning' in Godfrey, D. and Brown, C. (eds) *An ecosystem for research-engaged schools: reforming education through research.* Abingdon: Routledge, pp. 41–55.

Gough, D. (2013) 'Knowledge mobilisation in education in England' in Levin, B., Qi, J., Edelstein, H. and Sohn, J. (eds) *The impact of research in education: an international perspective.* Bristol: Policy Press, pp. 65–84.

Greany, T. (2015). 'How can evidence inform teaching and decision making across 21,000 autonomous schools?: learning from the journey in England' in Brown, C. (ed.) *Leading the use of research and evidence in schools.* London: Institute of Education Press.

Greany, T. (2017) 'Karmel oration: leading schools and school systems in times of change – a paradox and a quest', *Leadership for improving learning – insights from research: the Australian Council for Educational Research*

(ACER) research conference, Melbourne Convention and Exhibition Centre, Melbourne, 28–29 August.

Greany, T. and Earley, P. (2018) 'The paradox of policy and the quest for successful leadership', *Professional Development Today* 19 (3–4) pp. 6–12.

Hargreaves, A., Parsley, D. and Cox, K. (2015) 'Designing rural school improvement networks: aspirations and actualities', *Peabody Journal of Education* 90 (2) pp. 306–321.

Mincu, M. (2013) *Teacher quality and school improvement: what is the role of research?* [Online]. BERA inquiry paper 6. London: BERA. Retrieved from: www.bit.ly/2SaXjN2 [Accessed 4 December 2019].

Nelson, J. and Campbell, C. (eds) (2017) 'Evidence-informed practice in education: meanings and applications', *Education Research* 59 (2) pp. 127–135 [Online]. Retrieved from: www.bit.ly/31qIQkD [Accessed 4 December 2019].

Nelson, J. and Campbell, C. (2019) 'Using evidence in education' in Boaz, A., Davies, H., Fraser, A. and Nutley, S. (eds) *What works now? evidence informed policy and practice*. Bristol: Policy Press, pp. 131–150.

Nelson, J. and O'Beirne, C. (2014) *Using evidence in the classroom: what works and why?* Slough: NFER.

Nelson, J., Mehta, P., Sharples, J. and Davey, C. (2017) *Measuring teachers' research engagement: findings from a pilot study* [Online]. Retrieved from: www.bit.ly/2H5XGDP [Accessed 4 December 2019].

Nelson, J., Harland, J., Martin, K., Sharp, S. and Roy, P. (2019). *Formative evaluation of the North East primary literacy scale-up campaign* [Online]. Available: www.bit.ly/3bQfykc [4 December, 2019].

Nutley, S. (2013) 'Reflections on the mobilisation of education research' in Levin, B., Qi, J., Edelstein, H. and Sohn, J. (eds) *The impact of research in education: an international perspective*. Bristol: Policy Press, pp. 243–262.

Nutley, S., Powell, A. and Davies, H. (2013) *What counts as good evidence?* [Online]. London: Alliance for Useful Evidence. Retrieved from: www.bit. ly/2OswUcz [Accessed 4 December 2019].

Roberts, C. (2015) 'Impractical research: overcoming the obstacles to becoming an evidence-informed school' in Brown, C. (ed.) *Leading the use of research and evidence in schools*. London: Institute of Education Press.

Sharples, J. (2013) *Evidence for the frontline* [Online]. London: Alliance for Useful Evidence. Available: www.bit.ly/2OnP8Mo [Accessed 4 December 2019].

Stoll, L. (2015) 'Using evidence, learning and the role of professional learning communities' in Brown, C. (ed.) *Leading the use of research and evidence in schools*. London: Institute of Education Press.

Walker, M., Nelson, J., Bradshaw, S. and Brown, C. (2019) *Teachers' engagement with research: what do we know? A research briefing* [Online]. London:

Education Endowment Foundation. Retrieved from: www.bit.ly/2UqUxX4 [Accessed 4 December 2019].

Walker, M., Nelson, J., Smith, R. and Brown, C. (2020) 'Understanding the challenges for evidence-informed school improvement support in disadvantaged schools: an exploratory study' [Unpublished research report]. London: Education Endowment Foundation.

MAKING RESEARCH ENGAGEMENT A REALITY

GRAHAM HANDSCOMB *(graham@handscomb-consultancy.co.uk)*

Graham Handscomb is Visiting Professor at University College London (UCL) and was Professor of Education and Dean of The College of Teachers. He has had an extensive career of senior leadership of local authorities and schools and 20 years' teaching experience. He has championed the development of school-based practitioner enquiry and pioneered the concept of the research-engaged school.

LOFTY AMBITION AND DASHED HOPES?

For decades we have looked forwards to a time when, in schools up and down the country, teachers really become research engaged – when they use and apply research to establish genuine evidenced-informed practice. Indeed it feels as if this quest has created the mood music for much of my professional life! So, are we any nearer? Are we entering the era of the practitioner researcher and the age of the researching school?

Well, although it is too early to give an unqualified 'yes' with any great confidence, maybe there are some glimmers of hope. There appears to be a head of steam towards achieving this goal. Teachers are positive and schools supportive. Certainly, there are signs that Stenhouse's (1988) exhortation that 'it is teachers who, in the end, will change the world of the classroom by understanding it' is gaining some traction.

However, whilst it appears that the case for evidence use and practitioner research may have been won, we have still a long way to go. Teachers individually, and the profession in general, give warm welcome to the notion of using research evidence to inform, hone and improve teaching and learning. Yet this does not appear to be matched with any discernible impact on classroom practice or indeed on pupil outcomes. Instead we have the phenomenon of token assent with little actual change, of 'marshmallowy' intent with little follow-through or professional bite.

LITTLE CHANGE AND LIMITED IMPACT

Successive recent investigations by organisations like the National Foundation for Educational Research (NFER) and the Educational Endowment Fund (EEF) bear this out. They report that 'despite growing recognition within the teaching profession of the potential of research evidence in the classroom to support teaching and learning, embedding it into everyday practice is no mean feat' (Lord and Ward, 2019, p. 1). This NFER 'Literacy Octopus' project funded by EEF found few case study examples of schools using research-based materials or applying research evidence to practice.

The big concern is that even with positive teacher attitudes towards research use and practice, and with supportive schools, these are not in themselves sufficient factors and result in little actual impact on practice. This is borne out in Nelson and Walker's survey of evidenced-based practice (2019). They found that teachers report generally positive attitudes towards research evidence and that most teachers report that their schools offer supportive environments which enable evidenced-based practice to flourish. **But their main finding was that 'research evidence continues to play a relatively small role in influencing teachers' decision-making'** (Nelson and Walker, 2019, p. 1).

RESEARCH ENGAGEMENT – AN ENTITLEMENT

So what is causing such reticence? What is getting in the way? Why is there such a gap between what teachers do and what research suggests might provide effective ways to support student learning? Despite decades of well-meaning and growing interest within the profession in the use and application of research, why is there little change on the ground?

Well, this chapter will explore a number of factors. Prominent among these is the need for research use, application and practice to be much more at the heart of teachers' core outlook and day-to-day professional practice. It needs to be a dimension of their professionalism that is seen as crucial to the main business of teaching and learning; something that teachers care about and invest in because it resonates with teachers' fundamental purpose and values. Key to this is that it is seen as being something teachers embrace and choose rather than a worthy aspiration they are exhorted to adopt. Research needs to be seen as an important tool which teachers are keen to use because it empowers them and makes a difference to their practice.

All this indicates that research use needs to be founded upon a wholesale strategic approach to wider research engagement by both teachers and the schools within which they work. In an early report considering research engagement, Dyson (2001) identified three key dimensions:

- Teachers doing research – practitioner researchers
- Teachers using research – drawing on current thinking and learning from the external research community
- Teachers being part of research – being the site of research and part of the investigations of others

The last point relates to a school being sufficiently strategic in its research engagement to make informed prioritised decisions as to which research organisations it opens its doors to. Recently these three dimensions have been developed further as having a particular resonance with the school as a research-engaged eco-system (Godfrey and Handscomb, 2019).

Viewed in this light, the use and application of research is regarded less as something that a few are exhorted to do but rather as a core element of professional learning staff development programmes for all. Indeed it has been argued that this should be seen in terms of a fundamental professional expectation and right:

> *All teachers should have an entitlement to research training in order to develop their role as critical users of research ... All schools and colleges should have an entitlement, and perhaps a responsibility, to participate in a relevant research partnership for appropriate periods. (Dyson, 2001, p. 4)*

THE JOURNEY AND THE BATTLE

In a career that has spanned teaching and managing schools, leading local authority school improvement, and fellowships of many universities, including forging strategic school-university partnerships, my continuing mission has been to promote teachers' engagement with research.

It has been a hard battle! At the heart of the struggle has been the perceived tension with the standards and accountability agenda. Why should teachers – and indeed other staff – engage with and in research activity? With all the pressures and demands on teachers, is such involvement an indulgence they can ill afford? Laudable though reflection, enquiry and research are, is there not a danger that teachers will take their eyes off the ball of the main job of improving teaching and learning and raising standards? (Handscomb and MacBeath, 2008) Despite the growing evidence over a number of decades about the merits of a 'knowledge creating school' (Hargreaves, 1998) and the benefits of this for teachers' development of pedagogy (Baumfield and McGrane, 2001), encouraging teachers' use of research still tends to be perceived as a luxury – desirable but not essential (Handscomb, 2002; Handscomb, 2015).

Well, there is an increasing body of literature and school practice which indicates quite the contrary. Rather than being effete activities which divert energies from the school's core business, school-based enquiry and research are now being seen to make an important contribution to self-evaluation, improvement and the professional learning of staff (MacBeath and Mortimore, 2001). Engagement in and with research encourages practitioners to question, explore and develop their practice, making a significant contribution to improved teaching and learning. In fostering a school culture where teachers examine and critique their own practice, research activity can be an important and integral element of professional learning (Stoll et al., 2012).

A HOLISTIC APPROACH AND TEACHER POWER

All this debate and concern led me to help pioneer the concept of the 'research-engaged school' (Handscomb and MacBeath, 2003). This endeavoured to move beyond the notion of an isolated coterie of enthusiasts within a school to considering what it would look like for the organisation as a whole to have a commitment to research engagement – where research and its use became part of the pulse and life-force of the school community.

When the term 'research-engaged school' was first coined it was identified as having four inter-related dimensions: it would have a 'research-rich pedagogy' – that is, research would be manifest in the school's teaching and learning and classroom practice; it would have a 'research orientation' – exemplified in the school's values and culture; it would 'promote research communities' – within and beyond the school; and research would be at 'the heart of school policy and practice' (Handscomb and MacBeath, 2003).

Underpinning this entire approach was the conception of research in situ, borrowed from Stenhouse's definition of 'systematic enquiry made public' – i.e. where engagement with research by teachers is done with some rigour and also with transparency so that the process is shared as it proceeds. Indeed, the link with Stenhouse was a fundamental one because it resonated with his thinking about how using research was a core feature at the heart of the educational enterprise. It is all about knowledge, power and control. For Stenhouse, the stakes could not be higher and he inveighed against the way knowledge is used to subjugate rather than liberate both students and teachers. Research and enquiry were to be means of redressing this, establishing autonomy and redistributing control (see for instance: Stenhouse, 1975; Rudduck, 1988).

Thus, this call to arms was taken up years later when the term 'research-engaged school' was first coined (Handscomb and MacBeath, 2003). At that time we anticipated that 'the third millennium school is required to be self-evaluating, open to scrutiny, evidenced-based, data rich'; but, echoing Stenhouse, we suggested that nevertheless schools were often 'information poor':

> *This is, in part, because teachers feel no ownership of the data they are expected to use, nor is it necessarily data that they value … so teachers find themselves busy in implementation rather than inquiry, lacking in confidence to convert what they know or believe into a form that provides robust counter evidence, that speaks with conviction from teachers' own context and experiences.*
> *(Handscomb and MacBeath, 2003, p. 3)*

DOING AS WELL AS USING RESEARCH – SYMBIOTIC RELATIONSHIP

An essential part of this vision of empowerment is the notion of teachers as research practitioners – doing as well as using research. Two key features of a school's research engagement are how its staff use and apply the evidenced-based findings of others and also the degree to which they are enquirers themselves. Indeed, there are strong indications that there is a powerful relationship between the two. In fact this synthesising of the two elements has come to be seen as a core feature of later iterations of the 'research-engaged school' concept. So, for Wilkins (2011) the term 'research-engaged' entailed the practitioner combining the undertaking of one's own action research whilst concurrently accessing and making judicious use of published research.

The research learning community (RLC) model is particularly interesting in the way it is founded upon an approach where participants are asked to combine school-based knowledge from practitioner enquiry – on topics like growth mind-sets or effective grouping – with the insights of investigations from the wider external research community (Brown, 2017). One of the messages that emerged from the RLC initiative (Godfrey and Brown, 2019) was that there is a cathartic effect when teachers bring together their in-school research knowledge with research evidence from elsewhere. It is often in this context, in relation to their own enquiries, where teachers see the relevance and application of evidence from broader research.

What is evident from such initiatives is the way in which research engagement helps to instil in participants a greater sense of efficacy and agency (Durrant, 2014). Much of this is derived from the value of local knowledge, the potency of teachers who are closest to their classroom settings being the ones who conduct investigations into practice. What emerges as powerful is when such local knowledge is harnessed and utilised to problem-solve specific improvement issues, facilitated through enquiry communities like RLCs, and connected to wider research knowledge and social developments. So such 'local knowledge is understood to be a process of building, interrogating, elaborating, and critiquing conceptual frameworks that link action and problem-posing to the immediate context as well as to larger social, cultural, and political issues' (Cochran-Smith and Lytle, 1999).

MOVING RESEARCH INTO PRACTICE

So what is to be done? How can the gap between well-meaning intention and actually making a difference be bridged? How can research use and engagement become a reality within everyday practice? It is a daunting challenge given that after decades of promotion 'it appears that teachers typically view research evidence as a *nice to have*, rather than an *essential*, tool in their decision-making repertoire' (Nelson and Walker, 2019, p. 1). Well, exhortation, encouragement and support are clearly not enough in themselves – it is clear that positive climates alone are insufficient to change practice (Brown and Zhang, 2016). Such support will be effective when it is part of a phalanx of strategies within an integrated committed approach. Although Lord and Ward (2019) found few schools using research-based materials or applying research evidence to practice, there were exceptions. These were schools that 'already had in place a whole-school approach to research-engagement' and 'where in-school collaboration and support, and trying-out, reviewing and embedding the approaches seemed key' (p. 1).

It has been a long and often tortuous journey to promote research engagement that extends beyond the token and promotes evidenced-based practice which becomes part of the raison d'etre of the school. Reflecting on this mission it seems that what is required is a coherent combination of a number of ingredients:

Belief and courage

This is about the crucial importance of having the right disposition towards using research as a pivotal feature of one's professionalism. However 'disposition' is probably too anodyne a term. It could be argued that teachers have had this all along – a general, positive and welcoming disposition to research use, but little follow-through. What is needed is something significantly stronger. It's really about belief in the value of research and the potent contribution it can make. Then it's about courage to devote time and energy to it, even in the face of siren noises which raise the spectre of accountability and say that energies devoted to research use are an indulgence. This sense of fundamental belief and commitment, coupled with a tenacity of purpose that 'sticks with it' to gain the rich dividends of research engagement, is the key ingredient which all the others that follow below help to service.

Ethos and supportive culture

This was one of the core features identified within what it is to be a research-engaged school, and it remains an important ingredient in the promotion of evidenced-informed practice. Recent investigations into the use of research, mentioned in this chapter, stress that schools themselves need support in how to foster researching cultures. If established firmly then such positive cultures are vital in reinforcing and maintaining teachers' belief and continuing commitment to the research enterprise.

Structures and systems

Lord and Ward (2019) argue strongly that 'researchers and policy makers ... need to provide more opportunity and support for schools to build their capacity and have the appropriate systems and structures to engage with and use research evidence' (p. 1). Much of the literature on evidence-informed practice in schools emphasises that this will only become a reality when strong, clearly thought-through structures and systems are established. The effective contribution of such structures is that they forge clear integration between use of research and enquiry activity on the one hand, with school development and improvement processes on the other. 'This is because,' argue Brown and Zhang (2016), 'engagement with research evidence should not be something that occurs in isolation, rather it should be undertaken within the context of a wider iterative "cycle" of enquiry and improvement' (p. 4).

Leadership and empowering staff

Perhaps the most crucial factor in nurturing the belief and courage teachers need for sustained research engagement is the contribution of school leaders. Clearly they play a vital role in fostering supportive cultures and establishing structural frameworks for research engagement. But more than this, through their own participation in the use of research and through adopting an 'enquiry habit of mind' (Earl and Katz, 2006; Stoll, 2017), they model and mandate such activity, and lend it credibility and status.

Strategic 'informed' approach

Earlier in the chapter the case was argued for teachers' use of research to be embedded within a wholesale strategic approach to wider research engagement. Thus the school will have a joined-up strategy incorporating and coherently blending a range of involvement including: using research; having a rationale to determine which research investigations it agrees to participate in; and practitioners carrying out their own enquiries. This strategic approach is so important because there is a dynamic relationship between *doing* and *using* research which in turn relates to the important issue of teacher empowerment.

Indeed, this raises fundamental issues about the kind of terminology employed. A number of educationalists have questioned whether 'evidenced-based practice' is a neutral and value-free term. Hammersley (2001) examines the challenging process by which research is used and applied by practitioners, referring to 'problems in interpreting this evidence without background knowledge about the studies from which it arose' (p. 11). In setting out her five challenges in moving towards evidenced-informed practice, Stoll (2017) included thinking too narrowly about evidence and the dangers of being 'driven' by evidence. She argues powerfully for using the preferred term 'evidence-informed practice': 'If teaching is "evidence-informed" rather than "evidence-based", teachers are in the driving seat, not the evidence. This fits with another important feature of teacher professionalism – autonomy' (p. 1).

Skilling up and application

One of the vibrant messages that resonates throughout this mission to make research engagement in schools real and effective is the empowerment of teachers. Making sure teachers are well placed to be users of research means investing in their development and skill acquisition. Research evidence is not to be seen crudely as a cudgel to expose practice or as a universal panacea to be applied indiscriminately. If schools and teachers are to tap the richness of what research has to offer then this involves some serious attention to professional learning and resources that support this. Such provision might include, for instance, schools having better access to a robust evidence base like that held in academic journals or research databases and to user-friendly high-quality research syntheses (Goldacre, 2013; Brown and Zhang, 2016). Empowering teachers to apply research to their own professional contexts involves helping them acquire skills in the interpretation of research and providing practical support, guidance and strategies in carrying out their own enquiries (Handscomb, 2019).

RESEARCH AT THE HEART OF THE MATTER

This chapter began by striking a challenging note about the significant gap between aspiration regarding the striving for research-informed teaching and the limited extent to which this is happening to any degree or scale within schools. The good news is that there is every indication that the hearts and minds of teachers have been won over to this cause. It now remains to be seen whether, through a combination of strategic purpose and resolute follow-through, the dividends of research-informed practice will be realised. Above all, it is such an important goal because of the potential of research to empower and inspire teachers: 'Research leads teachers back to the things that lie at the heart of their professionalism: pupils, teaching and learning' (Rudduck, 2001, p. 1).

TOP TIPS

- Foster a dynamic relationship between *doing* and *using* research within the context of a research-engaged school.
- Emphasise evidenced-*informed* rather than evidenced-*based* practice.
- Move research into practice through a combination of ingredients: belief and courage; ethos and supportive culture; structure and systems; leadership and empowering staff; strategic informed approach; and skilling up and application.

REFERENCES

Baumfield, V. M. and McGrane, J. (2001) 'Teachers using evidence and engaging in and with research: one school's story', *British Educational Research Association Conference*, University of Leeds, Leeds, 13–15 September.

Brown, C. (2017) 'How to establish research learning communities', *Professional Development Today* 19 (2) pp. 30–55.

Brown, C. and Zhang, D. (2016) 'Is engaging in evidence-informed practice in education rational? What accounts for discrepancies in teachers' attitudes towards evidence use and actual instances of evidence use in schools?', *British Education Research Journal* 42 (5) pp. 780–801.

Cochran-Smith, M. and Lytle, S. L. (1999) 'Relationships of knowledge and practice: teacher learning in communities', *Review of Research in Education* 24 (1) pp. 249–305.

Durrant, J. (2014) '"Children see differently from us" – a fresh perspective on school improvement', *Professional Development Today* 16 (2) pp. 51–61.

Dyson, A. (2001) *Building research capacity.* Sub-group report chaired by Alan Dyson. Slough: National Education Research Forum.

Earl, L. and Katz, S. (2006) *Leading schools in a data-rich world: harnessing data for school improvement.* Thousand Oaks, CA: Corwin Press.

Godfrey, D. and Brown, C. (2019) 'Innovative models that bridge the research-practice divide: research learning communities and research-informed peer review' in Godfrey, D. and Brown, C. (eds) *An ecosystem for research-engaged schools: reforming education through research.* Abingdon: Routledge.

Godfrey, D. and Handscomb, G. (2019) 'Evidence use, research-engaged schools and the concept of an ecosystem' in Godfrey, D. and Brown, C. (eds) *An ecosystem for research-engaged schools: reforming education through research.* Abingdon: Routledge.

Goldacre, B. (2013) *Building evidence into education.* Department for Education. London: The Stationery Office.

Hammersley, M. (2001) 'Some questions about evidence-based practice in education', *British Educational Research Association Conference,* University of Leeds, Leeds, 13–15 September.

Handscomb, G. (2002) *Educational enquiry and research in Essex.* The Forum for Learning and Research Enquiry (FLARE). Chelmsford: Essex County Council.

Handscomb, G. (2015) 'Researching and learning collaboratively', *Professional Development Today* 17 (2) pp. 3–5.

Handscomb, G. (2019) 'Professional development though enquiry' in Godfrey, D. and Brown, C. (eds) *An ecosystem for research-engaged schools: reforming education through research.* Abingdon: Routledge.

Handscomb, G. and MacBeath, J. (2003) *The research engaged school.* Chelmsford: Essex County Council.

Handscomb, G. and MacBeath, J. (2008) 'The time has come for school-based research', *Principal Matters* (Winter).

Hargreaves, D. H. (1998) 'A new partnership of stakeholders and a national strategy for research in education' in Rudduck, J. and McIntyre, D. (eds) *Challenges for educational research.* London: Paul Chapman, pp. 114–136.

Lord, P. and Ward, N. (2019) 'How can we give evidence legs in the classroom? Learnings from the Literacy Octopus', *NFER Blog,* 30 January. Retrieved from: www.bit.ly/31zIUhN [Accessed 28 October 2019].

Nelson, J and Walker, M. (2019) 'Evidence-informed approaches to teaching – where are we now?', *NFER Blog,* 13 May. Retrieved from: www.bit.ly/31wcCED [Accessed 26 October 2019].

MacBeath, J. and Mortimore, P. (eds) (2001) *Improving school effectiveness.* Buckingham: Open University Press.

Rudduck, J. (1988) 'Changing the world of the classroom by understanding it. A review of some aspects of the work of Lawrence Stenhouse', *Journal of Curriculum and Supervision* 4 (1) pp. 30–42.

Rudduck, J. (2001) 'Teachers as researchers: the quiet revolution', *DfES/TTA Conference,* Queen Elizabeth II Conference Centre, London, 7 March.

Stenhouse, L. (1975) *An introduction to curriculum research and development.* London: Heinemann.

Stenhouse, L. (1988) 'Artistry and teaching: the teacher as focus of research and development', *Journal of Curriculum and Supervision* 4 (1) pp. 43–51 .

Stoll, L. (2017) 'Five challenges in moving towards evidence-informed practice', *Impact* (interim issue). Retrieved from www.bit.ly/38GOphD [Accessed 28 October 2019].

Stoll, L., Harris, A. and Handscomb, G. (2012) *Great professional development which leads to great pedagogy: nine claims from research*. Nottingham: National College for School Leadership.

Wilkins, R. (2011) *Research engagement for school development*. London: Institute of Education Press.

USING EVIDENCE FOR IMPROVEMENT
HOW CAN THE EDUCATION ENDOWMENT FOUNDATION'S
TEACHING AND LEARNING TOOLKIT HELP?

STEVE HIGGINS *(@profstig)*

Steve Higgins is Professor of Education at Durham University. A former primary school teacher, he is passionate about the use of evidence from research to support decision-making in schools. He is the lead author of the EEF's Teaching and Learning Toolkit and is interested in understanding how best to engage with policy-makers and education practitioners to ensure the use of evidence is effective.

INTRODUCTION – TACKLING CORE CHALLENGES

This chapter looks at the Education Endowment Foundation's (EEF) *Teaching and Learning Toolkit* and the potential contribution it makes to research-informed teaching. The chapter will outline the *Toolkit*'s challenges of making evidence both accessible and accurate in a way that they are sufficiently actionable to ensure improvement. Publishing summaries of evidence doesn't automatically lead to schools improving their teaching practices. Sometimes people misinterpret what you intended. I've heard accounts of schools devoting extra hours to marking pupils' work under the impression that this would deliver effective feedback. This approach focuses on feedback delivered, but not on whether the feedback was received, understood and acted upon by the learner. On one occasion, we suggested that reducing class sizes is only moderately effective and very expensive, so not cost-effective as a strategy to help learners. One local authority in Scotland tried to use the *Toolkit* as justification for increasing class sizes, ignoring the finding that pupils in larger classes tend to do a little bit less well, on average. These challenges of synthesis and its interpretation are at the heart of research-informed teaching.

THE EEF'S *TEACHING AND LEARNING TOOLKIT*

The *Toolkit* was originally funded by the Sutton Trust to summarise evidence from educational research to challenge thinking about effective spending for the pupil premium policy in England. This policy aimed to increase spending in schools to benefit children and young people from disadvantaged backgrounds. The *Toolkit* was subsequently adopted by the EEF and is now in widespread use in England with just under two-thirds of headteachers saying they consult it (National Audit Office, 2015). Similar approaches to evidence synthesis and translation, and adoption of evidence in policy-making, are growing in popularity, reflecting a global movement towards more effective engagement with research and evidence.

In the *Toolkit*'s approach, an inventory of interventions or programmes is created and categorised in terms of the evidence for their effectiveness, cost and impact. The aim was to create something like a *Which?* consumer guide for education research, covering topics of interest and relevance to policy and practice. The UK government cited the *Toolkit* as an exemplar for its new network of What Works centres – for policing, early interventions, ageing – alongside those already established for health and education (Cabinet Office, 2013). This commitment to spend public money on the most effective practices is impressive, but the 'What Works' label can imply a certainty that I believe oversimplifies what the research means. Research can only tell us what has worked in the past, not what will work in the future. Indeed, I argue it can only offer indications of what may work under certain conditions.

The *Toolkit* website (Education Endowment Foundation, 2018) summarizes the messages across different areas of education research with the aim of helping education practitioners make decisions about supporting their pupils' attainment in schools. It is designed to be accessible as a web-based resource for practitioners. It uses meta-synthesis as the basis for the quantitative comparisons of impact on educational attainment. This is where the findings from different meta-analyses are combined to give an overall effect. This is similar to, and was inspired by, Hattie's (2008) approach in *Visible Learning*. The aim of the synthesis is to provide information and guidance for practitioners who are often interested in the relative benefits of different educational approaches, as well as information from research about how to adopt or implement a specific approach. What distinguishes the *Toolkit* is the inclusion of cost estimates for the different approaches to guide spending decisions along with an indication of the robustness of the evidence in each area.

BANANARAMA: IT AIN'T WHAT YOU DO; IT'S THE WAY THAT YOU DO IT

The Bananarama principle is named after the pop group Bananarama due to their 1982 hit single with Fun Boy Three, 'It Ain't What You Do....'. (Most people smile at the reference but even if they don't, the song is something of an earworm and tends to stick in your head!) It is an important principle for research-informed teaching when acting on the findings of research. The initial point was a simple one: it wouldn't be what schools spent, but the way they spent the pupil premium that would get results (Major and Higgins, 2019). The deployment of teaching assistants, reducing class sizes and ability grouping are all examples of the Bananarama principle. The principle underscores the power but also limitations of evidence in helping a teacher decide what to do in a classroom; how an approach is implemented is vital and just as important as its content. This principle reflects the spread of findings in each area of the *Toolkit*. Evidence can be helpful, but it is never going to be enough. Put more formally, the Bananarama principle also reflects a statistical argument. The range of effects within a *Toolkit* strand is greater than the difference between neighbouring strands. This suggests that although people have been successful (or unsuccessful) on average when adopting an approach, there is also a spread of effects that we should take into account. The *Toolkit* only tells us what has worked from other studies 'on average' and contains all of the statistical risks of averaging averages involved in this kind of synthesis. I think of this evidence as providing practitioners with a 'good bet' for what is likely to be successful or unsuccessful in a new context, based on how large the average effect is, represented as the average months' impact icon, as well as the spread of the effects, which gives an idea of the riskiness of the bet.

We also have to remember that average impact in these studies is based on a comparison with a control group or 'counterfactual' condition (Higgins, 2018). In averaging the effects, we 'average' the comparison conditions. As we become more certain that something is likely to be effective, we become less certain about what it is actually better *than*. This is important because an already highly effective school is likely to be better than the 'average' comparison or control school. Any typical gains found in research may well be harder to achieve in an already successful classroom or school. Overall, the larger the effect and the narrower the spread of effects, the more likely the average is to be useful in other contexts. The smaller the average effect and the wider the spread of effect, the riskier it becomes.

YOU NEED TO KNOW WHAT TO STOP AS WELL AS WHAT TO START

This line of reasoning also suggests that we need to be clear about what we should *stop* doing. Whenever schools adopt something new, they must stop doing something else. There is little or no spare time in schools. We rarely reflect on this, so it can be hard to tell what gets squeezed out when we start something new. Research can also help us think about this, by providing information about things that have not worked, or tend not to work so well, on average. Research has clear limitations in its specific applicability. It tells what's worked, on average and over there, for someone else; it does not tell us what will work *here*. It is only once we understand these limitations that we can use it appropriately. This can be easily forgotten in the debates over 'what works' which can so easily become polarized between extreme positions. Indeed, I find the 'What Works' label problematic as I explain later in the chapter.

In the debates, we often talk about what is effective and what are effective approaches based on research evidence, but perhaps we should also start to focus on what is efficient. We might choose a particular approach not because it is more effective than another, but because it takes less time, or requires less preparation and marking by the teacher, or improves pupils' social skills as well as curriculum outcomes. We certainly should be wary of 'effective' approaches which demand more time, as something will be pushed out or have to be squeezed in to less time in the rest of the school week.

PARTNERSHIP BETWEEN RESEARCH AND PRACTICE

My work in developing the *Toolkit* with the EEF and trying to communicate what I think it means to teachers has led me develop a model which represents my understanding of this challenge. Some of the responsibilities in the model are from the perspective of the researcher (see figure 1). These involve the research being **accessible**, **accurate** and **actionable**. This immediately sets up a series of tensions for the researcher, represented by the connecting lines in the diagram, to summarise findings **accurately** but succinctly in a way which educational practitioners can understand and put into practice. 'Accuracy' refers mainly to how findings are summarised in relation to what was found (answering the question 'Did it work there?' or addressing the internal validity of the study).

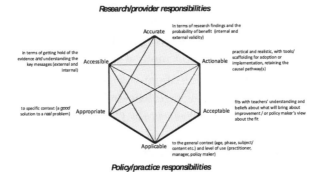

Figure 1: A model of research and practice responsibilities in research adoption and application

Understanding how research might be relevant in a new context is problematic in education. This is not least because we have almost no replication in education research and the samples of schools, teachers and pupils are not randomly selected. It is therefore hard to estimate how likely it is that an approach might be equally successful somewhere new. We know that **accessibility** is a key issue both in terms of getting hold of research evidence, but also in terms of understanding it. One of the main drivers behind the development of the *Toolkit* website was to create an **accessible** but **accurate** resource for education professionals. Academic journal articles are constrained by genre, form and the history of the discipline, and are rarely an easy read for the busy teacher.

How you distil findings into **actionable** steps is even more challenging. I've likened this before to picking the strawberries out of the jam (Higgins, 2018). You can sometimes see that the fruit is there, but it is so boiled and crystallised by the meta-analytic jam-making process that it no longer looks or tastes like strawberries!

From the practice perspective, I believe there are also responsibilities in terms of the research being **applicable**, **appropriate**, and **acceptable**. A good fit between research evidence and the practice context is essential, but I think this needs to be the responsibility of the teacher or school as they best understand how to meet the educational needs and develop the capabilities of their pupils. It is important to know that it is likely to be applicable in terms of subject, age and approach. One of my worries about research from fields other than education is being clear about how the findings might apply in a classroom and a specific curriculum context. Psychology research on motivation and neuroscience research into brain function are not directly applicable, though the findings often appear seductively suitable. When these findings are tested in the classroom, they may not always have the effects expected (Bowers, 2016; Lazowski and Hulleman, 2016).

It is important to identify whether research is **appropriate** for the particular teacher and the pupils involved. To increase the chances of it being appropriate, I think it should meet an identified need or a perceived problem, rather than being plucked from the top of a list of effective strategies or chosen at random from successful research findings. Identifying a problem or challenge is more likely to create a match between the new setting and the research context where it successfully made a difference. It is likely to replace problematic practice that needs improvement, rather than replacing something at random, which may be working well.

One way of looking at the *Toolkit* is as an encyclopaedia of solutions to educational challenges which others have found in the past. The extent of the impact and distribution of the effects gives you a probability of how likely it is to be useful in the future. The problem is that the actual questions to which we have all of these answers are no longer attached as they are buried in the original research. It is therefore important to consider whether a particular research-based practice is **appropriate** as a solution to the challenges a particular school or teacher faces.

The final practice dimension is how **acceptable** the findings are. At one level, they have to be educationally acceptable. Some kinds of behavioural change may be very efficiently achieved with pain or discomfort, but they would not be educationally or ethically acceptable. The next level is more difficult to address. To stand a chance of being successful in supporting change, research findings have to be acceptable to the teachers involved. If the findings conflict with deeply held beliefs about effective practice then they may either be rejected and not attempted, or even adopted resentfully and set up to fail. I have always argued that, as a classroom teacher, if you presented me with a robust and rigorously researched reading intervention which was consistently successful when evaluated, I could make it fail in my classroom, guaranteed. Teachers are the gatekeepers of their own practice.

There is an irony here that I have experienced in working with various teachers and schools. The teachers who are more open to research-based approaches often appear to me to be the ones who are already highly effective. They actively seek to improve their practice and to increase the range of strategies they have available to address the teaching and learning challenges that they face. They are eager to try out approaches backed by research. By contrast, I feel that sometimes those I think might benefit most from trying out such strategies are perhaps the ones most likely to find them unacceptable. There is a technical issue here too, which deepens the irony. Schools and teachers who are achieving results which are above average may find there is less benefit from something that works 'on average'. By contrast, schools which are performing less well are more likely to see larger gains than average as they are starting from a lower base.

CONCLUSION

We need to be clear about the limitations as well as the potential benefits of research-informed practice. Research can understand patterns of effects and help us identify 'good bets' based on the accumulation of findings across studies.

The applicability of these findings is then problematic as we cannot be sure how these general findings apply to a specific context or a particular class of learners. The findings are likely to be helpful, on average, across a large number of classes and schools, but this may not help an individual teacher or a particular school to identify what will work for them.

This suggests that research-informed practice should be a partnership between researchers and practitioners where each partner takes responsibility based on their professional expertise. The *Toolkit* aims to offer an overview of the relative benefits of different areas of education research. It does not and cannot give precise recommendations for research-based practices to an individual teacher.

TOP TIPS

- Start with a problem or a challenge you'd like to solve. You are more likely to find a solution from research which will help improve learning outcomes for children and young people.
- Think about what you will stop doing. How will you create the space to do what you think will help?
- Remember the Bananarama principle: it ain't what you do; it's the way that you do it! You will need to commit to the solution you have chosen and watch out as you develop it to make sure it is actually helping.

REFERENCES

Bowers, J. S. (2016) 'The practical and principled problems with educational neuroscience', *Psychological Review* 123 (5) pp. 600–612.

Cabinet Office (2013) *What Works Network* [Online]. www.bit.ly/2S5sE4U

Education Endowment Foundation (2018) *Teaching and Learning Toolkit* [Online]. Retrieved from www.bit.ly/2RUkdZ6 [Accessed 30 October 2019].

Hattie, J. A. (2008) *Visible learning: a synthesis of over 800 meta-analyses relating to achievement.* Abingdon: Routledge.

Higgins, S. (2018) *Improving learning: meta-analysis of intervention research in education.* Cambridge: Cambridge University Press.

Lazowski, R. A. and Hulleman, C. S. (2016) 'Motivation interventions in education: a meta-analytic review', *Review of Educational Research*, 86 (2) pp. 602–640.

Major, L. E. and Higgins, S. (2019) *What works? Research and evidence for successful teaching.* London. Bloomsbury.

National Audit Office (2015) *Funding for disadvantaged pupils.* Department for Education. London: National Audit Office.

SCHOOL-BASED RESEARCH FOR CONTINUOUS QUALITY IMPROVEMENT

RAPHAEL WILKINS *(raphaelwilkins66@gmail.com)*

Raphael Wilkins was formerly Pro Director (international consultancy and knowledge transfer) at the Institute of Education, University College London. He began his career as a secondary teacher, then entered local authority education administration before moving into higher education.

In this chapter I argue that there has never been a more propitious time for school-based research engagement to benefit the teaching profession, the quality of school education, and the well-being of the communities schools serve. But to realise those benefits, the conceptualisation and practice of school-based research need to evolve.

A PERSONAL JOURNEY

I was in mid-career as a local authority Director of Education, and already with some experience of national roles, when I first discovered the teacher practitioner research movement. That encounter in about 1998 changed how I thought about education policy and leadership. It seemed to offer an approach to the development of teachers and schools which was truly aligned with educational principles, and a welcome counterbalance to the political micro-management of school practice by the New Labour government which had been recently elected. I had the pleasure of working with some of the pioneers of teacher-led school development (Frost et al., 2000) and of the concept of the research-engaged school (Handscomb and MacBeath 2003). I initiated some school-based research projects among the schools for which I was responsible, and commenced my doctoral research which featured case studies of school leaders who had promoted research engagement by teachers as a key element of their approach to school leadership.

Next, during a freelance stage, and while completing my own research, I undertook long consultancies with the Local Government Association and with the General Teaching Council for England on matters relevant to the school-based research agenda, and I worked with schools and teachers in support of university-accredited programmes of school-based research engagement. I moved to a full-time university appointment in 2006, and shared that journey of exploration in Wilkins (2011).

My work became increasingly international; and within that, two strands had a bearing on how I thought about school-based research engagement. First, I learnt about the range of conditions and expectations within which teachers worked in other countries. That showed (among other things) how the hostile and distrustful stance of successive UK governments towards the teaching profession has been atypical globally. Secondly, a number of my projects concerned the professionalisation of teaching, including advising on development through 'national college' structures and through teacher licensing schemes. In the UK, as president of the College of Teachers, I actively supported the replacement of that body by the creation of the Chartered College of Teaching.

A CLIMATE HOSTILE TO AGENCY AND REFLECTION

I agree with other contributors that the spread of school-based practitioner engagement with research over the last 20 years has been disappointing. The truth may be even worse than the impression, because I suspect that those within the practitioner research community talk disproportionately with each other, especially at conferences. From my other work with schools, there seem to be plenty where none of the staff have heard of it; plenty where headteachers do not particularly like their staff to think for themselves; and plenty of staffrooms ready to sneer at a teacher wishing to improve themselves. The systemic factors responsible for this are clear; I shall also argue, perhaps more controversially, that the practitioner research community has in some ways circumscribed itself more narrowly than necessary.

The systemic constraints have included arrangements for the pre-service education of teachers and the award of qualified teacher status which have done little or nothing to inculcate an expectation of career-long research engagement, or indeed professional development more generally. 'I am fully qualified to do my job; why should I have to do anything more?' is a stance encountered quite commonly.

Secondly, over the period in question, the inspection criteria used by Ofsted took no specific account of a school's professional development culture, nor even, it might be argued, of whether school managers treated their staff caringly as human beings. Instead, 'strong' leadership was praiseworthy, even where it was experienced as the kind of unsupportive bullying blame culture which drove significant numbers of teachers out of the profession in their first five years. I found that widespread leadership style repulsive because it is so contrary to the core educational purpose of a school. No one wants to buy perfume at a counter where the staff are unwashed and stinking; no one will buy into joy in learning in a school where teachers are allowed no agency, but instead are looking over their shoulders fearfully.

The third systemic constraint has been the disconcerting extent to which government ministers have felt free to express opinions about, and seek to influence, the details of classroom practice. 'Disconcerting' because educators of my generation were assured during our formative years that such a thing could never happen in England, that following the defeat of fascism in Europe, checks and balances were built into the English system to provide permanent cushioning between the education professional and the elected politician (Alexander, 1954). What is the point of investing time and effort in the long-term research-informed evolution of practice in a climate of whims and fashions?

RESEARCH ENGAGEMENT FOR PROFESSIONALISATION

Little wonder, then, that the school practitioner research movement has not gained greater traction; praise and appreciation are due to those many who have persevered. Of course, it has not been an undifferentiated 'movement'; within a broadly common overall organising philosophy it takes different forms and reaches different levels of development according to context, and is driven by a range of motivations. Somewhere near the centre of my own mind map of it are teachers undertaking small-scale research projects as part of externally accredited courses, usually higher degrees. There may be a group of them in the same school, supporting each other. That mode of professional development may be actively enabled and promoted by senior management, who may also arrange for staff more generally to access professional reading and to discuss what research has to say about issues the school is dealing with. The school may draw upon the national infrastructure of 'knowledge wholesalers' digesting academic research for practitioner consumption.

I have worked with the whole range of school personnel and with teachers of all subjects and phases. It is hard to summarise without drawing caricatures, but my impression is that special schools have had the most conducive conditions for research engagement. They have much more professional discretion, are small, used to multi-professional working, generate a lot of student data, and have to tailor-make their methods. In secondary schools, the picture is mixed: the bulk of what is seen as research-engagement may be qualitative, and while contributed from all faculties, the methodology may sit most comfortably with teachers strong in social science and humanities. Research engagement only thrives where it is supported by middle and senior leaders, and it takes place predominantly in schools which are both successful and stable. In the most successful and confident examples, school leaders value the maintenance of their professional development culture more highly than achieving a particular Ofsted grade. They are the exception, and generally schools in challenging circumstances see (an entirely false) dichotomy between fire-fighting and research engagement, and prioritise the former. Except where research engagement is truly embedded into school culture, it is transient: the champions move on; interest wanes after the degree has been achieved. These comments are my personal impression; for a thorough and insightful analysis, see Godfrey and Brown (2019).

To make substantial progress, something different is needed. When the Chartered College of Teaching was established, one of my valedictory hopes for it was that when the time was right, it would hammer out with government a working agreement of the following form: 'These are matters of education policy which are the concern of government; these are matters of education practice which are the concern of the teaching profession.' Although such a treaty is long overdue, I say 'when the time is right' because the deal cannot be struck until the teaching profession displays arrangements and working practices which do credibly offer quality assurance and continuing quality improvement. That is the path which other professions have had to trea:, first to assert themselves in relation to government, and then to become the senior source of expertise. At present, universities accredit professional development programmes in education, whereas in the mature professions, the professional body accredits the university degree.

To take the first steps on that journey towards professional recognition, it is essential that evidence-informed practice becomes the norm across the entire teaching work of a school. A teacher not research-engaged would be like a driver not looking at road signs; but that does require a re-think about 'research' because the kind of research needed for professionalisation is professional research rather than academic research. The key distinctions between the two are that professional research operates within a different ethical framework, counts professional judgement as valid evidence, and stands separately from academic levels of assessment.

RESEARCH ENGAGEMENT FOR TOTAL QUALITY

When people describe what research engagement is going on in their school, they tend to omit the analysis of attainment data. Indeed, they may even imply that the 'standards agenda' is somehow oppositional to research engagement and evidence-informed practice. That is strange: the systematic collection and analysis of attainment data, and its use in lesson planning and individual academic tutoring, is clearly a good example both of research and of evidence-informed practice which is going on in most schools in the country. Assessment for learning is both research and evidence-informed practice. Teachers research every time they assess their students' work, assuming that they intend to learn from the assessment and apply it to future teaching tactics.

These are examples of professional research, like the specialised journalist researching their topic, or the serious novelist researching context, or the biographer researching their subject. They do it to make sure their work is good and will withstand scrutiny. I chose those examples because teachers need knowledge of their subject, their context, and the lives of their students. I avoided examples of professional research from law and medicine because there is no pedagogic equivalent to case law and clinical records, although Fenwick and Nerland (2014) draw interesting comparisons about how professional learning is changing across a range of professions. They emphasise that professional learning is increasingly globalised, online, and networked – trends I explored in Wilkins (2014). Purposeful, structured, critical professional reading is research. So is getting other people's perceptions, whether through peer review or student feedback. So is a quest to deepen understanding or gain fresh insights through experiences, such as when a year 6 teacher gains first-hand experience of what is going on in year 7, or when teachers do charitable work in a school in a third-world setting during the summer vacation.

The concepts of quality assurance and improvement are quite helpful in illustrating the value of professional research. Near to the heart of any system of quality assurance is the following sequence of questions in relation to any activity:

- Are there clear standards?
- How and by whom are those standards set?
- How and by whom are those standards monitored?
- How and by whom is performance evaluated against those standards?

If those questions are applied to students' progress in core subjects, most schools will be able to point to quite robust arrangements for managing quality. What about other areas, including those often featuring in the all-important mission statement? 'Our students are happy': oh really? What is the evidence and process for judging that? 'We have excellent relations with parents': so were they involved in that assessment? 'We enable our students to achieve their full potential': who dares to define, and hence limit, what any particular young person growing up in the modern world will be able to achieve? In all these cases, progressing from sentimental aspiration (or self-delusion) to quality professional practice involves researching the perceptions and experiences of students, parents, staff, and community stakeholders.

RESEARCH ENGAGEMENT FOR THE FUTURE DEVELOPMENT OF THE SCHOOL SYSTEM

Quality assurance is not just about fitness for purpose now, but also capacity to respond to change. Some depictions of school research engagement, especially of the 'what works' variety, imply that its purpose is to enable teachers to become smarter and more effective at what they are doing now in the system as it is. There is nothing wrong with refining methods, except where the implication is that that ought to be sufficient, that the system itself does not need to evolve. Yet the aims, values and expectations of teaching have evolved greatly: compare the present to the days when teachers used fear and punishment to prepare children for their predetermined station in life. The pace of change will increase; young people themselves are driving that. It is right that teachers, as a profession, consider how the aims and methods of teaching, and the role of school in society, may evolve over the next few decades.

To that end, conceptual research is important: the development of new ways of looking at things. Often, the questions addressed through empirical research are generated by that. A good example is the mass of empirical research in the fields of equalities and inclusion, which has been prompted by the conception of new paradigms and meta-narratives: new ways of seeing what goes on in the world, and how things ought to be. Conceptual research involves reading widely, pondering deeply, networking actively with people in contrasting contexts, and being open to having one's beliefs, assumptions and priorities challenged.

In Wilkins (2014) I argued that if education aims to help people to make informed choices about what they do now, and what they plan to do in the future, then learner agency must be at the heart of pedagogy. If pedagogy is to harmonise formal learning in school with the informal learning permeating all other parts of young people's lives, it must to some extent understand and embrace the issues important to students and their communities. The notion of an activist curriculum should be decoupled from its Marxist roots and applied in an objective and professionally defensible manner, building on the work of Oyler (2012). Thus research-engagement becomes part of pedagogy, in which teachers and students co-research issues that affect students' sense of agency.

Research-engagement for future quality also has organisational implications. School leaders may see 'their' school as tightly knit, like a living organism, like a regiment oozing with esprit de corps. Professional research will reveal a range of perspectives. If a school community has 600 members, the one place will be perceived and experienced as 600 different spaces. For a long time in public discourse, the unit of competition and comparison has been the 'school' as a de-personalised administrative unit. Good schools already have porous walls and an external orientation. The more that teaching becomes professionalised and research-engaged, the stronger teachers' external moorings and sources of professional identity will become: through subject and phase associations, peer review groups, community partners, links to external sources of expertise, and informal social media networks. Gradually the school building may come to be seen as the serviced premises in which self-reliant and self-motivated teachers happen, for the time being, to be practising their profession. For school leaders supporting increased research engagement, one of the hard steps may be discerning when to lead, when to support, and when to let go.

TOP TIPS

My advice to teachers who would be research-engaged:

- Recognise how much professional research you do already and do it more consciously.
- Research your students' and colleagues' perceptions and learn from them.
- Network widely and preferably internationally.
- Think long and hard about the kind of significant long-term change you want to work towards.

REFERENCES

Alexander, W. (1954) *Education in England: the national system, how it works*. London: Newnes.

Fenwick, T. and Nerland, M. (eds) (2014) *Reconceptualising professional learning: sociomaterial knowledges, practices and responsibilities*. London: Routledge.

Frost, D., Durrant, J., Head, M. and Holden, G. (2000) *Teacher-led school improvement*. London: RoutledgeFalmer.

Godfrey, D. and Brown, C. (eds) (2019) *An ecosystem for research-engaged schools*. London: Routledge.

Handscomb, G. and MacBeath, J. (2003) *The research engaged school*. Chelmsford: Essex County Council.

Oyler, C. (2012) *Actions speak louder than words: community activism as curriculum*. New York: Routledge.

Wilkins, R. (2011) *Research engagement for school development*. London: Institute of Education Press.

Wilkins, R. (2014) *Education in the balance: mapping the global dynamics of school leadership*. London: Bloomsbury.

WHAT CAN 400 SCHOOLS TELL US ABOUT RESEARCH-INFORMED TEACHING?

MARIA CUNNINGHAM *(@mcunners)* **& DAVID WESTON** *(@informed_edu)*

Maria Cunningham is Head of Education at the Teacher Development Trust. She leads TDT's work to support schools with auditing the quality of their CPD, teaching and learning and Department for Education (DfE) funded school improvement programmes.

David Weston is CEO of the Teacher Development Trust, co-author of *Unleashing Great Teaching* and Chair of the Department for Education's CPD expert group.

There is a difference between thinking that you have a good CPD programme and actually knowing that you do. It's even harder to know if it's having an impact on learners in the classroom. In this chapter, we explore findings from over 400 schools, ranging from infant schools to colleges, academy trusts, independent schools, special schools and international schools. At each school, the Teacher Development Trust carried out an in-depth diagnostic review of the processes, culture and leadership of professional development, with whole-staff surveys, interviews and examination of paperwork.

From this evidence base, we found that the more that teachers are drawing from the world of educational research, the more they are able to strengthen their understanding of how students learn and use evidence to inform their teaching. Yet it is a school's wider systems and processes which will allow this approach to become truly embedded and enacted by all, instead of just a proactive few.

RESEARCH, INNOVATION AND EVIDENCE

The first element to explore is how well the school engages with research to underpin its decision-making. We might look, for instance, at the school development plan. To what extent are priorities set with reference to key research? Are they evaluated in ways that draw on evidence-informed assessment tools? Are interventions and expert partners chosen on the basis of research?

For example, one school's focus on literacy was underpinned by an initial diagnostic reading assessment using a carefully validated and research-based test across each year group. Interventions were then carefully matched to the findings. Another school overhauled its performance management process after reading a systematic review of the latest evidence about effective appraisal and goal-setting.

Staff notice when leaders model the use of research in their own decision-making. It encourages a culture of critical thinking, where research is something that *everyone* uses, rather than something that is cherry-picked and imposed.

The next area to consider is whether individual staff engage with research. This includes exploring the extent to which staff members have access to research summaries and digests, and whether they have opportunities to work with researchers and higher education institutions. At Falinge Park High School in Rochdale, a teaching and learning team run research briefings every Tuesday evening after the normal school day has finished. In each session, the work of a key education researcher is summarised, then the findings are discussed in subject teams, examining how the ideas might relate to each teachers' own pupils. Staff have access to further reading – accessible summaries plus original papers – and topics are picked up later within staff members' structured enquiry into their own practice.

KNOW WHAT YOU ARE TRYING TO ACHIEVE

Drawing from the evidence base helps leaders and teachers to make more informed decisions about what to do to improve outcomes. Helpfully, resources such as the Education Endowment Foundation (EEF) *Teaching and Learning Toolkit* increasingly allow practitioners to make best bets about the potential impact of various interventions on students. However, successful practical application also requires a careful diagnosis of what the pupil need is in the first place, and the very same principle must apply when planning professional learning for staff.

We found that schools with the strongest professional development programmes systematically analyse their training needs across three levels, starting with the end in mind and using a variety of evidence sources to align:

- whole school priorities
- team (department, phase or faculty) priorities and
- individuals' needs.

When thinking about improving teaching and learning, we recommend that leaders keep two key questions at the front and centre of their planning;

- What are the intended impacts from our CPD programmes?
- How will we know if we've met these aims?

Figure 1 is a table taken from a shared organisational 'vision' document produced by leaders at Rossett School in Harrogate, where the formative and summative evaluation of CPD is an integral process for all staff as they progress through their learning. Evaluation is framed as the process of checking that the school's CPD programme meets its objectives in the best way possible.

Evaluation level Based on Guskey (2000)	What is measured?	How will we evaluate this?
Participant reaction	Initial satisfaction with experience	Questionnaires/surveys Focus group discussions CRCs (collaborative research communities) informal feedback
Participant learning	New knowledge and skills of our teaching staff	Performance management and appraisal (BlueSky) Faculty TeachMeets CRC sessions Observations/demonstrations T+L (teaching and learning) journal
Organisational support/challenge	The organisation's (Rossett School) support and facilitation	Focus groups/interviews Teacher Development Trust CPD Audit Performance management and appraisal (BlueSky)
Participants' use of new skills and knowledge	Quality of implementation	Questionnaires/surveys Faculty TeachMeets Faculty T+L meetings Observations/video Student feedback/interviews
Students' learning outcomes	Students' learning outcomes (performance and attainment, attitudes, participation, skills and behaviour)	Student interviews Attainment data Pastoral data Student work Lesson study research

Figure 1 – A table demonstrating how CPD evaluation is implemented at Rossett School, Harrogate

Staff are always informed of or involved in identifying the intended aims of CPD, meaning that needs analysis and evaluation go hand in hand. Throughout the year, colleagues take part in collaborative research communities (CRCs) and optional complementary CPD sessions which are designed to involve a range of evaluative activities. This helps individuals to understand and break down the impact of their CPD at a range of levels, and to inform next steps accordingly.

WHERE TO FOCUS

Although schools have traditionally favoured CPD related to generic pedagogy, recently there has been growing recognition of the importance of teachers' subject knowledge and their understanding of how generic CPD can be contextualised to respond to specific learning issues in the subjects they teach. This has become even more of a priority in light of recent updates to the Ofsted inspection framework, which put renewed focus on subject leadership and curriculum design. Research tells us that schools in which opportunities are carved out for both generic and subject-specific pedagogy are more likely to improve student outcomes (Cordingley et al., 2015).

In practice, this means that teachers should be encouraged to plan in time – without guilt – for developing their subject knowledge, just as they would be for marking or moderation. At Notre Dame High School in Norwich, for example, leaders restructured their timetable to eliminate less effective meetings and limit administrative or procedural conversations to email. They reallocated this time (a total of nine hours per year) to collaborative subject-specific CPD, in which groups of staff now focus on a particular pupil learning issue (or 'threshold topics') related to subjects that they would like to improve, e.g. concept variation in maths or developing enquiry skills in history. At subsequent teaching and learning meetings, colleagues then combine pedagogic and subject knowledge and share across departments how they have implemented strategies in their classrooms, and also explore how this might be adapted or trialled by different departments. Colleagues we interviewed felt this to be a 'hugely beneficial use of time' which 'enables better sharing between teams' and 'gives the teachers the opportunity to contribute' to the planning and design of CPD.

Enabling subject teams to make links with subject associations such as STEM, the Institute of Physics or the Geographical Association, to name just a few, can be a particularly powerful way to drive this even further. Middle leaders frequently tell us that their departments do have existing group memberships which, sadly, are not fully utilised. Some useful ways to make the most of the resources on offer could be for lead practitioners to circulate subject publications or specific articles within them, or to signpost colleagues towards training opportunities.

CULTURE AND CHANGE

Using research to change teaching requires a culture of collaboration and trust. A key lesson from successful schools is that leaders need to deliberately focus on creating a professional environment where collaboration and openness thrives.

This is underpinned by research on teacher development. Kraft and Papay (2014) found that, in schools where teachers kept improving, the professional environment was particularly conducive to collaboration around improving teaching practice. Teachers had plenty of opportunities to meet and discuss lesson planning, assessment and curriculum. In these effective schools, teachers also reported much higher levels of trust in their peers, with a real shared sense of mission to do everything possible to help pupils learn.

When we analyse this element in schools, we explore attitudes to professional development. Is it seen as an activity just for sharing ideas, or is it seen as a tool to help teachers meet pupils' needs? Are staff empowered to try out new approaches they learn, or are they risk-avoidant? Do staff members feel comfortable thinking critically about each other's practice, or are they too afraid to be seen as impolite?

At Barrowford Primary School in Lancashire, leaders have taken a number of approaches to building collaboration. Some approaches are more formal, such as using lesson study and providing regular group supervision sessions for teachers to reflect. Others are more informal, ensuring that middle leaders create spaces where staff can share ideas. One teacher, when interviewed, described the 'real sense of team' that had been deliberately fostered.

INTERNAL VS EXTERNAL EXPERTISE

If raising the quality of teaching means bringing evidence-informed practice into the classroom, then this by extension involves looking outwards. Engaging with external expertise allows both exposure to the latest research and support in translating this effectively into the day-to-day. It also offers new perspectives and can disrupt the current thinking or beliefs of staff. It is important that staff are sufficiently challenged, both to catalyse their own learning and to sustain their engagement with their practice.

In the muddy marketplace of training provision for schools, it is so important to ensure that all colleagues are drawing from content that is informed by a robust evidence base, not being tempted by the consultant making the boldest claims. At Norbriggs Primary School in Chesterfield, commissioning is a key strength. We observed that 'external provision is chosen with precision using collaborative approaches to help make informed decisions. Only training providers who value pupil needs, staff needs and high-impact evidence-informed approaches are considered.'

In the best schools, there is an organisation-wide culture of constructive challenge based in evidence, such that teaching staff are confident in constructively critiquing their colleagues. When engaging with a CPD provider, leaders check that they are clear in setting out the why and request that any background reading is provided to both them and the participants. We constantly remind schools not to be afraid but to be reflective and critical in ensuring that any claims being made by providers about good practice are actually valid and up to date – this should never be an after-thought!

PROCESSES AND STRUCTURES

To bring all of the elements together requires some careful thought about systems and leadership. In the most effective schools we visit, the leadership of teaching, learning and professional development is distributed. Key stakeholder groups can include:

- Senior leaders – ensuring that the whole of the SLT sees teaching quality and evidence as their role, not just one member
- Middle leaders – leaders of professional learning in each of their areas, with their most important task being growing the capacity and knowledge of staff in their teams

- Teaching and learning teams – a dedicated group of experienced and expert practitioners who have been trained to support others using methodologies such as coaching and lesson study while helping them engage critically with research

In schools where this works well, leaders work hard to ensure that all meetings are focused mainly on sharing knowledge and collaborating to improve practice, rather than on administrative issues and briefing. This is true of whole-staff meetings (which are repurposed where possible as professional development) as well as of middle-leader meetings (which become joint planning and discussion, along with curriculum planning and moderation).

CONCLUSION

So, what have 400 schools told us about research-informed teaching? We've found that it's as important to think about people and culture as about processes and resources. Updating professional practice requires trust and time. It's a process of change which affects individuals, teams and organisations. Bringing research into schools is necessary, but not sufficient.

Ultimately, schools can only improve when the practice in them improves. Our key message is this: school leaders need to take the leadership of staff learning just as seriously as pupils' learning. When schools become great learning environments for adults, everyone will benefit – pupils, staff and wider society.

TOP TIPS

- Start with the end in mind. Once intentions for teachers and pupils have been defined, design flows naturally and it's much easier to gather evidence of change.
- Do a few things well. Choosing three priorities allows you to sustain focus on these areas and to develop a clearer vision for professional development.

- Infuse your school with ideas. Find ways to connect with specialist expertise – e.g. from the Chartered College of Teaching, subject associations, research schools and local networks – or coordinate carefully structured peer visits with other schools.

REFERENCES

Cordingley, P., Higgins, S., Greany, T., Buckler, N., Coles-Jordan, D., Crisp, B., Saunders, L. and Coe, R. (2015) *Developing great teaching: lessons from the international reviews into effective professional development* [Online]. Retrieved from: www.bit.ly/36XNsiY [Accessed 4 December 2019].

Guskey, T. R. (2000) *Evaluating professional development.* Thousand Oaks, CA: Corwin Press.

Kraft, M. A. and Papay, J. P. (2014) 'Can professional environments in schools promote teacher development? Explaining heterogeneity in returns to teaching experience', *Educational Evaluation and Policy Analysis* 36 (4) pp. 476–500.

FACILITATING
COLLABORATIVE INITIATIVES

ANDREW MORRIS *(@andrewmorrised)*

Originally a physics teacher in FE, Andrew Morris subsequently became a deputy director of City and Islington sixth form college. Keen to make research evidence more influential in teaching, he worked as a research manager for FE, then as the Director of the National Education Research Forum. In his current role as chair of the Coalition for Evidence-Based Education he works on practical projects linking research, policy and practice.

INTRODUCTION

Teachers make crucial classroom decisions on a minute-by-minute basis and, unusually amongst the professions, they mainly do so alone. A multiplicity of ideas and influences shape these decisions – previous experience, peer influence, government regulations and inspectorate expectations. Somehow, evidence from research has to find its way into the mix.

The means by which such evidence reaches the practitioner is, at least in England, haphazard; and the tools needed to put it to use, under-developed. The various bodies responsible for setting the research agenda, producing research, developing useful materials from it and using them to improve practice add up to a kind of ecosystem. This chapter is about efforts to develop collaboration across the poorly connected parts of this ecosystem.

Paradoxically, perhaps, the argument is not itself based on research evidence. It is notoriously hard to demonstrate rigorously that the use of research evidence in teaching leads to better outcomes for learners. This chapter is purely narrative – a reflection on a selection of initiatives at local and national levels with which I have been involved throughout my career as teacher, college leader, research manager and, ultimately, reformer. Better to skip this chapter if you are looking for effect sizes or a systematic review! A strange thing to find oneself saying, given how important they both are.

LOCAL LEVEL
Tackling a number of hurdles
Very immediate challenges lie at the heart of projects based in local provider organisations – schools, colleges, early years and adult education settings. It may prove difficult to enthuse colleagues to engage with research at all; and of those that do engage, few feel they have sufficient time to read the existing evidence beforehand. The need for understanding of a range of methodological options and relevant theory presents a further challenge.

Many institutions have solved the first problem by starting small, often through the enthusiasm of an individual research champion and by working closely with an issue that is salient at that moment. Where this proves fruitful and manageable, others may join in once the idea has proved beneficial. For example, a small infant school took this approach when deciding how to respond to lower performance identified in data on reading compared to other areas. Three teachers looked into the research evidence, selected and tried out new approaches and evaluated them. The following year other teachers were persuaded and the governing body and parents became seriously interested subsequently.

The second challenge – skills and knowledge – is often met by working in partnership with external researchers. There are various models for this. In a curriculum project I co-led in London in the 1990s,[1]

---

1. Papers from the Hamlyn Unified 16+ Curriculum Project (1992–4) at the Institute of Education, University of London available from the author.

an academic and I, then a college leader, co-designed the overall project framework, based on theoretical and practical considerations, while practitioners proposed mini-projects based on issues they saw as directly important to them. The projects, on topics as diverse as careers education and block timetabling, were carried out by practitioners while academic researchers monitored, advised and ultimately evaluated these. In a later project in Warwickshire (Merrill, 2000), college practitioners devised and carried out projects and met together for discussion with academics who also produced theory-based papers relevant to the projects.

In these and other cases, the full potential of collaboration was not realised because of the relative distance between the two communities and a reluctance to find a middle way in which the two types of contribution could be combined. Practitioner work tended to be localised to the context in which it was carried out with insufficient recourse to generalisable theory, whilst the academic outputs went largely unread within the wider practice community.

Practitioner ownership and support

A specific scheme at the Further Education Development Agency addressed this disconnect by bringing together people from multiple colleges with a university through the Learning and Skills Research Network (Morris and Norman, 2004). The approach proved effective because practitioners designed and carried out research and managed projects on issues of their own choice, with inputs from the universities on methodology and existing literature. Analyses were carried out jointly and outputs communicated locally and nationally. Its limitations, however, centred on the brief one-year lifetime of projects, dictated by the annual nature of government funding and on the scattergun approach to selection of topics.

Practitioner-researchers and research champions in schools and colleges tend to see the support and recognition offered by their senior team as crucial. Capacity for research is severely inhibited where this is absent (Coldwell et al., 2017). Studies of the role of senior teams in fostering a research culture (CEBE, 2019) suggest that they can make a difference by modelling research use themselves, ensuring research evidence is brought to bear on routine activities such as SMT and governors' meetings and in professional and organisational development.

In an effort to reduce the cultural separation of researcher and practitioner, I worked on ways to intensify the degree of collaboration. In one city-wide project aimed at reducing bullying, initiated by the local authority in Coventry (Rickinson et al., 2009), a number of interventions had been planned by practitioners as part of the city's strategy for schools. These plans were subsequently enhanced by the addition of a peripatetic researcher who travelled around the participating schools advising on each stage in the process – defining the question, consulting the literature, designing the intervention and evaluating its effects. The approach not only dramatically bolstered the teachers' sense of professionalism and confidence but also, through engaging them with the literature, led them to modify the design of the interventions – to good effect. A city, region or locality may offer a helpful framework within which specific policies, on issues such as bullying, are funded.

Other models build in explicit research training for practitioners as they work alongside full-time researchers. This was an approach used effectively in a project, Transforming Cultures in FE,[2] in the ESRC Teaching and Learning Research Programme in the 2000s. Project funding enabled the practitioners to be released from frontline duties to contribute their experiential knowledge to an empirical study based on theoretical insights in sociology. A more systemic training approach is the Education and Training Foundation's Practitioner Research programme[3] for the FE and skills sector. Practitioners with proposals for action research are offered a short residential training experience plus individual coaching with established university researchers as they develop and implement their action research ideas. Over many years, this

---

2. TLRP Transforming Research Cultures project (2005–2008) papers available at www.bit. ly/2SKGDN1 JW: This link said the service was 'temporarily unavailable' when I tested it just now. I've kept the URL on the assumption that it will become permanently available by the time we go to press, but we'll have to check later.

3. Education and Training Foundation Practitioner Reseach Programme. See www.bit. ly/2tGbiCm

effective method has seen the gradual development of a research-capable community whose graduates go on to energise networking activity across the country.

The challenges of collaboration

These examples of locally based practitioner research collaborations demonstrate something of the range of approaches that can be taken and suggest some of the benefits and drawbacks of so doing. But there is a further consideration: what can we learn about the way in which successful collaborations form in the first place?

There are many challenges. Individual practitioners' concepts of research may differ radically according to the discipline or vocational area in which they themselves have been educated. Preconceptions about qualitative and quantitative approaches or views about what researchers refer to as 'epistemology' (the theory of knowledge), for example, may lead to initial clashes that take time to resolve. Peers attempting to collaborate between schools or colleges that are in effect competing for students may be more interested in guarding successful ideas than sharing them. And, of course, the perennial issues of shortage of time and absence of leadership support may affect any project plan.

Collaboration between academia and practice faces even tougher challenges, with the conflicting pressures of those who need to work and publish within their academic discipline and those who need to bring home something of more immediate practical value for the organisation that employs them.

A comparative study within the European EIPPPE network[4] in the 2010s considered forms of collaboration between schools and universities over the use of evidence (Morris et al., 2018). By combining experiential knowledge of different schemes in several countries with theory-based models of knowledge exchange, it developed a way of analysing the process and made proposals about effectiveness. The most important of these was that, from the very outset of a collaboration, all parties need to fearlessly confront the actual situation on the ground. This can be very

---

4.   Evidence Informed Policy and Practice in Education in Europe website www.eippee.eu/cms

challenging where current practice is threatened, as it was in a case in the study involving mainstreaming of special needs pupils in rural Sweden. Time taken to confront differing perceptions at an early stage pays off in the long run as the parties work out, in an atmosphere of equal regard, how their respective types of knowledge can be combined to best effect.

NATIONAL LEVEL
The need for coherence
At national level, the fragmented pattern of responsible bodies has resulted, historically, in lack of coherence in the planning and funding across the research ecosystem as a whole. Academic studies are commissioned in one arena, applied research in others; knowledge for practice is mobilised for schools separately from colleges and evidence for the training of teachers and leaders in yet others. Professional development activity, which should be a key conduit for the application of evidence to practice, is not organised as a system at all. This degree of incoherence redoubles the importance of collaborative approaches to research and evidence use, at least to minimise duplication and at best to widen the scope of research and increase its impact on practice.

The incompatibility between the rapidity imposed by short-term funding and the slower processes of academia makes a combined assault on the lack of useful classroom knowledge difficult to pull off. With the publication of the 1998 Hillage report, which took a critical look at England's educational research system (Hillage et al., 1998), and the publication of *What Works* in 2000 (Davies et al., 2000), it became clear that similar deficiencies extended across the entire education system – and indeed, beyond to other sectors.

Strategic initiatives to make progress
The National Education Research Forum, set up in response to the Hillage report, enabled the idea of collaboration to be applied not to research itself, but to activities aimed at improving the wider knowledge system within which research sits. As a place for the research, policy and practice communities to debate system improvements, the Forum

failed to make significant progress. It demonstrated, rather than resolved, the many challenges it was set up to address. Valuable papers were produced on fundamental issues such as research capacity, funding and impact and on options for a national evidence centre with 'development and research' programmes to supply it, but action to follow it up stalled. Government, academics and the Research Council proved unable to develop a more integrated system and a Funders' Forum likewise failed to develop a more coordinated agenda for commissioning. There was insufficient trust about the legitimacy of the process and the chance of high-level collaboration melted away as the parties continued to dispute.

A programme of development activities, however, based on practical issues such as developing an evidence portal and encouraging evidence use in schools and colleges did manage to make progress. Representatives from leading organisations in research commissioning and production, teacher development, teacher training, curriculum development and policy development proved willing to overcome their differences. In this spirit of collaboration, they worked together with teachers, leaders and professional associations in the context of practical action. Independent, third-party chairing and championing were critical factors in this.

The NERF initiative was followed by a Strategic Forum for Research in Education, set up in 2008 by two research bodies to review the 'system for the provision and use of knowledge' (Pollard and Oancea, 2010). Through its conferences and papers, it further clarified issues but gained equally little traction with policymakers and decision-makers in the long run.

Building on the lessons of both these national initiatives, Jonathan Sharples and I, with the support of the Institute of Effective Education, set up the Coalition for Evidence-Based Education.[5] The CEBE approach added to the work of previous initiatives by seeking to foster collaborative activity through practical projects rather than abstract debate. Despite being an unfunded network of voluntary collaborators, CEBE has outlived all previous initiatives and developed a number of

5.   See CEBE website: www.cebenetwork.org/what-cebe

significant projects over the ten years of its existence. In the **Education Media Centre**,[6] journalists, researchers and publishers work together to enhance the role of research in media reporting. **Evidence for the Frontline** provided an online question-and-answer service for school teachers about the evidence base for specific classroom issues, and **Leading Research Engagement** offered practical guidance to support research leads in schools and colleges. **Evidence and Leadership** explores the role of leaders in fostering a culture of research use within their organisations, and **Assessing Claims in Education** draws on work in the healthcare sector to offer practitioners advice on how to judge claims about research evidence.

These collaborations, once again, demonstrate the willingness of individuals in universities, schools and colleges, foundations, research institutes, training and support bodies and media organisations to work together, often without recompense, in order to make progress on the many weak links in the knowledge ecosystem. On the downside, such voluntaristic, pioneering projects remain fragile and relatively short-lived, only able to impact at scale, as and when funding bodies choose to put their weight behind them. On the plus side, it is possible to argue, though not to prove, that small-scale initiatives of this kind may, nevertheless, affect the general climate, thereby encouraging gradual progressive change in the organisations that participate.

CONCLUSION – TOWARDS A MORE INTEGRATED SYSTEM?

In my experience, the principal challenges to efforts to connect research, practice and policy are best understood as cultural rather than instrumental. The resistances to change are deep and the reform processes slow. Habits, attitudes, beliefs, incentives and rewards dominate all our ways of being and working and these differ significantly between communities. Collaboration is a social process, involving actors with quite different backgrounds, offering distinct sets of skills and under differing pressures; this can slow things down and lead to extra costs. Effective collaboration often seems to rely on the presence of an independent

---

6.   See EMC website: www.educationmediacentre.org

third party or broker capable of steering the diverse parties though their wrangles – and there's evidence to back this up (OECD, 2007).

With the recent rise in availability of evidence-based guidance, a new challenge arises as it is forced to compete with the plethora of other types of guidance with which teachers and their leaders have to contend daily. Practitioners and other decision-makers are having to judge which sources can be relied upon and which come top in the competition for attention.

These doubts, new and old, herald a new phase in the maturation of the evidence movement. In any area of science, leading-edge research is a subject of controversy; different studies reveal different aspects of a problem. Some may appear contradictory, at least in the short run; much of it may be inconclusive, from a practical point of view. But research marches on and, as multiple sources of evidence begin to accumulate, a degree of clarity may emerge as seems to be the case today in areas such as formative assessment and metacognition. Other areas remain unresolved.

A fundamental issue that remains more or less untouched as yet is the paucity of evidence on teaching and learning in subject and vocational areas outside the core subjects and also on pastoral and other non-academic aspects of learning. While academic research in the disciplines of sociology, economics and psychology throws light on crucial issues of equity, economic effectiveness and cognitive capacities in general, there is much less investment in research on specific approaches to, say, how best to teach gravitational theory or run a geography field trip, let alone on tutorial grouping or careers education. It's as though doctors had plentiful evidence on germ theory but precious little on how to treat malaria, specifically.

Education still lacks an NHS-type structure to commission research on the specifics of teaching and an NIHR (National Institute of Health Research)[7] analogue to link together basic science, applied science and practice development. The Education Endowment Foundation is making great advances on the former of these in relation to school teaching, but achieving a more integrated system will require an extension across the whole of education and coordination with the work of research

7.   See NIHR website: www.bit.ly/2voTqML

councils and major foundations. These and other important issues have been identified in a significant report (Royal Society and the British Academy, 2018) which proposes a body to debate research priorities and develop research strategies, involving researchers, practitioners and policymakers, and argues for a better geographical spread of research capacity to facilitate collaboration between the research and practice communities. Let's hope this call, mirroring that from NERF 20 years earlier, will hit the right political moment and be realised.

TOP TIPS

- Envisage research as a social process involving relationships with others.
- If you want to make a difference, engage from the outset with those whose help you'll need later.
- Work on a topic close to your experience but also of value to others.
- Use research reviews to discover what others have found before you.
- Allow plenty of time to prepare before, and communicate after, your main study and enjoy these stages too.

REFERENCES

CEBE (2019) *The role of leadership in fostering a culture of research and evidence use*. Retrieved from: www.bit.ly/39T7j4V [Accessed 10 November 2019].

Coldwell, M., Greany, T., Higgins, S., Brown, C., Maxwell, B., Stiell, B., Stoll, L., Willis, B. and Burns, H. (2017) *Evidence-informed teaching: an evaluation of progress in England*. Department for Education. London: The Stationery Office. Retrieved from: www.bit.ly/2UDWeAl [Accessed 14 November 2019].

Davies, H. T. O., Nutley, S. M. and Smith, P. C. (2000) *What works? Evidence-based policy and practice in public services*. Bristol: Policy Press.

Hillage, J., Pearson, R., Anderson, A. and Tamkin, P. (1998) *Excellence in research on schools*. Research report No. 74, Department for Education and Employment. London: The Stationery Office.

Merrill, B. (2000) *The FE college and its communities*. London: FEDA. Retrieved from: www.bit.ly/31HK1My [Accessed 14 November 2019].

Morris, A. and Norman, L. (2004) *Collaborative research in practice*. London: Learning and Skills Research Centre.

Morris, A., Sigurðardóttir, A. K., Skoglund, P. and Tudjman, T. (2018) 'School–university knowledge-exchange schemes', *Research for All* 2 (1) pp. 62–72. Retrieved from: www.bit.ly/2SgMVVA [Accessed 12 November 2019].

Rickinson, M., Batch, L., Bell, L., Blinco, V., Brundrett, D., Chapman, B., Edwards, S., Johnson, T., Perkins, A., Russell-Dudley, D., Scott, P. and Waters, J. (2009) *Tackling bullying, using evidence, learning lessons.* Reading: Education Development Trust. Retrieved from: www.bit.ly/2vS5qqq [Accessed 13 November 2019].

OECD (2007) *Evidence in education: linking research and policy.* Paris: OECD.

Pollard, A. and Oancea, A. (2010) *Unlocking learning? Towards evidence-informed policy and practice in education.* London: Strategic Forum for Research in Education.

Royal Society and British Academy (2018) *Harnessing educational research.* Retrieved from: www.bit.ly/38LFfjK [Accessed 10 November 2019].

UNDERSTANDING WHAT WORKed
LEARNING THROUGH PRACTITIONER INQUIRY

VIVIENNE MARIE BAUMFIELD (*@CRPL_Exeter*)

Vivienne is Professor of Education and Director of the Centre for Research in Professional Learning at the University of Exeter, UK.

INTRODUCTION

I currently co-direct a research group focusing on professional learning within and across different professions; prior to taking up my first post in a university, I was a secondary school teacher in the North East of England. My interest in the relationship between teaching and research began when I enrolled on a postgraduate certificate in education (PGCE) programme after four years of doctoral study in Indian philosophy. I found learning to be a teacher – as I grappled with how to make sense of the purpose of education, curriculum development, pedagogy, and assessment whilst also building positive classroom relationships – more intellectually challenging than completing my doctorate. It was, therefore, surprising to encounter attitudes to teaching that underplayed, if not explicitly denied, the importance of engaging with research in the development of teacher knowledge. After 12 years working in inner-city secondary school classrooms, I became a teacher educator in a research-intensive university. The change in role only confirmed my conviction that binary oppositions of theory and practice were misleading and unhelpful; teaching is a research-and-evidence-informed profession.

Individual teachers make a difference; in fact, as the work of school improvement researchers has shown, the effect of individual teachers was the cause of up to 75% of classroom-level variance in pupil performance (Muijs and Reynolds, 2002). Outcomes such as this have driven interest in finding the most effective way of supporting the development of teachers, but we are still some way from reaching agreement as to what this might look like. One of the barriers has been a difference of opinion as to what the work of being a teacher actually entails; and as this drives our view of what they need to know (and how they can learn what it is that they need to know), this lack of consensus matters (Zeichner et al., 2015). We can improve the situation by seeking better understanding of what might at first appear to be opposing points of view, such as the often-polarised 'what works' debate.

TEACHER PROFESSIONALISM: UNDERSTANDING 'WHAT WORKed'

Focusing on 'what works' is associated with an instrumental view of teachers' work and the promotion of a technical-rationalist approach to teacher development. It is an association often seen as being in opposition to the idea of being a reflective practitioner and, therefore, diminishing the professionalism of teachers. In fact, a concern to test an idea by seeing whether it is useful in real classroom settings is an integral element of critical reflection on practice and of any claim to be a professional. The problem is not basing decisions on 'what works'. What can undermine professionalism is reliance on external prescription without being able to evaluate its relevance to the context of the teacher's own classroom. Given the complexity of what happens in classrooms and the powerful effect of context on outcomes, teachers play an important role in mediating research and their perspective should be valued. Lawrence Stenhouse, an early advocate of the importance of teachers as researchers, characterised the relationship of academic research to teaching as offering intelligent propositions to be tested in action (Stenhouse, 1975). If this relationship is to reach its full potential, teachers need to be confident in their ability to interpret research, they need to develop research literacy, and they need to work closely with academics who are willing to listen. Policymakers play a crucial role in facilitating productive relationships between researchers and teachers; they determine expectations and can support or hinder collaboration through the management of working conditions.

The need to encourage researchers, policy makers and teachers to work together if education systems are to improve has long been recognised and was the focus of a major international review nearly 20 years ago. *Knowledge Management: New Challenges for Educational Research* (OECD, 2003) commended the English education system for the work that had begun to support research and development (R&D) through a number of initiatives designed to strengthen teachers' capacity to carry out research and to work in professional partnerships with academic researchers. However, the review also recognised that there were no quick solutions as any change would require sustained effort and a long-term strategy – not least because what was required was a major knowledge and cultural change in the practice of teachers, researchers and policy-makers.

> *Teachers need to look beyond their schools for evidence and think rigorously about their practice. Policy-makers need to 'value' and apply research evidence in their development of policy and implementation. Researchers must work more closely with teachers to continuously improve the knowledge base on education practices and 'what works' (use-inspired basic research). (OECD, 2003, p. 18)*

Since the publication of the review, much has changed but not necessarily in ways that have sustained the required shift in culture. The work of the Education Endowment Fund, the *Teaching and Learning Toolkit* and the establishing of research schools support aspects of the original project to build capacity within the education system; but integrating the interests of the different communities requires fundamental changes that have yet to be realised.

Focusing on teachers' professional learning (what teachers know, how they know and what they need to know) offers a way of thinking about different forms of knowledge and the consequences for the relationship between practice and research. Rather than advocating research as something external to teaching that teachers 'use' or which some teachers might 'do' as a bolt-on activity, we can ask how their understanding of what has worked and not worked in the classroom contributes to a body of knowledge for, in and of practice (Cochran-Smith and Lytle, 1999) that any claim to be a profession requires. Recent analysis of the characteristics of professionalism emphasises the importance of knowledge creation and integration within 'epistemic cultures' (Jensen et al., 2012); the following section explores the role school-university research partnerships play in the development of teaching as a 21st-century profession.

WORKING IN A COMMUNITY OF INQUIRY: SCHOOL-UNIVERSITY RESEARCH PARTNERSHIPS

Partnership between schools and universities is frequently invoked as a panacea for educational problems but with considerable variation in views as to what a school-university partnership might involve, resulting in disappointment and unfulfilled potential (Dyson, 1999; Greany et al., 2014; Handscomb et al., 2014). Schools and universities have common educational interests on which they work together – to address widening participation of under-represented groups and to attract more students to study science, technology, engineering and maths (STEM) subjects, for example. Faculties of education in universities and schools are closely connected through initial teacher education (ITE) and teachers' continuing professional development (CPD). All of these aspects have a research dimension and in each area of activity there has been a shift in the relationship, 'so that the focus is on partnership and collaboration rather than assuming that theoretical knowledge is exclusive to the university sector' (Baumfield and Butterworth, 2007, p. 412).

In 2014 Research Councils UK and the National Co-ordinating Centre for Public Engagement commissioned the School-University Partnership Initiative (SUPI) learning project with the aim of learning from existing work on school-university partnerships and exploring the potential for a programme of work to enhance quality and impact (Greany et al., 2014).

The SUPI report concluded that whilst working in partnership offered real benefits, finding practicable and sustainable ways of achieving these remains elusive. It is argued in this chapter that there are two aspects to the problem. Firstly, the breadth of scope in what is included in studies of school-university partnership militates against achieving depth of understanding of key factors, and analysis of the work of a specific form – school-university *research* partnerships – has been under-represented. Secondly, the persistence of a dominant paradigm in which knowledge is 'produced' and 'applied' underplays the role of inquiry in a process of learning and, in professional learning in particular, as a powerful driver for research that is collaborative and generative.

Interest in the potential of school-university research partnerships gained momentum in England in the period following a number of reports highlighting what was considered to be a damaging gap between educational research and the practice of teaching (Hargreaves, 1996; Tooley and Darby, 1998; Hillage et al., 1998). In 1997, the Teacher Training Agency (TTA) with the Centre for British Teachers (CBT) launched a multi-site school-based research consortium (SBRC) programme, which aimed to:

> *Improve the accessibility of the existing stock of knowledge; improve the quality and relevance of research; help teachers play a more active role in conceiving, implementing, evaluating and disseminating research. (TTA, 1996, p. 1)*

Four SBRCs – each comprised of a group of schools, a local education authority (LEA) and a university – were funded for three years in what has been described as an 'experimental laboratory for policy' (Kushner et al., 2001). The School University Partnership for Educational Research (SUPER) was established by researchers in the Faculty of Education at the University of Cambridge and a group of local headteachers in 1998.[1] The experience of the SBRC and the early days of establishing SUPER demonstrated that whilst reconfiguring structures and relationships

---

1.   See www.bit.ly/2UAC4r0

between academic researchers and teachers is challenging, it can be done, and important lessons were learned. The fundamental principle is to find a shared interest in understanding a problematic situation, and this is not difficult to do when the focus is on classrooms and finding ways of improving the educational experiences of students. Inquiry is the trigger; as the rocket scientist Wernher von Braun pointed out, 'research is what I do when I don't know what I am doing'. And it is the desire to find solutions that promotes collaborative effort. It does not mean that what is already known is ignored; nor is it about re-inventing the wheel. But the experience of school-university research partnerships suggests that engaging *in* research through inquiry supports engaging *with* research. The process of professional learning through inquiry is consistent with what we know about the importance for workplace learning of unsettling the established ideas and bringing in new perspectives to make matters of fact matters of concern (Fenwick, 2014). More detailed discussion of the work of the SBRC and SUPER is not possible here but the key points can be summarised as follows:

- Teachers need access to tools for inquiry that can be integrated into their daily teaching practice.
- School leadership needs to promote a 'safe to fail' environment to support responsible experiments in practice.
- Opportunities to work collaboratively, within and across schools, are essential to teachers' professional learning.
- Powerful professional learning environments require people with a diversity of expertise and perspective with a common interest in addressing real classroom situations. (See McLaughlin et al., 2015).

The principle of positioning research at the centre of professional learning through collaborative inquiry continues to inform the work of centres such as CollectivEd[2] and the Centre for Research in Professional Learning[3] amongst others.

---

2.   www.bit.ly/2tGPQx4
3.   www.bit.ly/31GCHAN

MAKING A DIFFERENCE

Participation in a school-university research partnership creates a community of inquiry within which a common language for research develops. Deliberations on a shared interest in resolving a problematic situation heightens awareness of research as a complex process and sustained reflection on methodology and the weight of evidence. It amounts to nothing short of the re-professionalisation of teaching as evidence-informed. As the external evaluation of the SBRC concluded: 'Based on this alone there would appear to be promise in the sponsorship of teacher/university networks' (Kushner et al., 2001, p. 60).

The biggest difference that school-university research partnerships make is in re-energising the teacher-student relationship as the excitement of transacting learning and understanding of learning in the classroom is kindled. Inquiry opens up learning so that problems are interesting rather than threatening and participants speak of the wow factor as they make new discoveries. It is not uncommon for everyone involved to emphasise that it is a re-discovery of why they came into education in the first place.

It would be misleading to suggest that working in school-university partnerships does not present difficulties. Working across institutional boundaries puts a strain on resources and relationships and can be hard to sustain over long periods of time. Tensions also arise around the reconciling of what is learned from close study of specific contexts, what is termed 'ideographic' research and what has more general resonance (Elliot, 2001); and between what participants themselves find convincing and what they think will convince others (Baumfield and McGrane, 2001. But these are not issues confined to working in partnership, and indeed such ways of working can contribute to wider debate on the nature of evidence.

The greatest success I have experienced as a participant in school-university research partnerships is the devising of simple tools to support pedagogical inquiry that yield profound effects. I have written elsewhere about the impact of the community of inquiry as a vehicle for promoting learning as an inclusive, educative experience (Baumfield et al., 2009;

Baumfield, 2015) and it lends itself equally well to the professional learning of teachers and academics.

CONCLUSION – USING PAST LEARNING TO FORGE NEW POSSIBILITIES

The 21st-century teacher can draw upon a wealth of experience relevant to the development of teaching as a research-informed profession. In order to reap the full benefits of what has gone before, we need to overcome the adverse effects of a tendency to forget what has gone before and the confusion of terms and labels that obscures what approaches may, or may not, have in common. Access to what we have already learned needs to be improved but there should also be opportunities to test and discover new possibilities. Working together can help us to question what has *worked* – how and for whom – and propose new intelligent proposals to be tested in action.

TOP TIPS

- Build on what we know from the work of school-university partnerships to make optimal use of existing links between schools and universities.
- Encourage policymakers to recognise the importance of spaces for inquiry in professional learning.
- Promote the sharing and development of tools for pedagogical inquiry.

REFERENCES

Baumfield, V. M. (2015) 'Mind the gap: theory and practice in professional learning', *Professional Development Today* 17 (2) pp. 8–17.

Baumfield, V. M. and Butterworth, M. (2007) 'Creating and translating knowledge about teaching and learning in collaborative school–university research partnerships: an analysis of what is exchanged across the partnerships, by whom and how', *Teachers and Teaching: Theory and Practice* 13 (4) pp. 411–427.

Baumfield, V. M. and McGrane, J. (2001) 'Teachers using evidence and engaging in and with research: one school's story', *British Educational Research Association Conference*, University of Leeds, Leeds, 13–15 September.

Baumfield, V. M., Hall, E., Higgins, S. and Wall, K. (2009) 'Catalytic tools: understanding the interaction of enquiry and feedback in teachers' learning', *European Journal of Teacher Education* 32 (4) pp. 423–35.

Brown, C., (2019) 'School/university partnerships: an English perspective', *Die Deutsche Schule* 111 (1) pp. 22–34.

Cochran-Smith, M. and Lytle, S. L. (1999) 'Relationships of knowledge and practice: teacher learning in communities', *Review of Research in Education* 24 (1) pp. 249–305.

Dyson, L. L. (1999) 'Developing a university-school district partnership: researcher-district administrator collaboration for a special education initiative', *Canadian Journal of Education* 24 (4) pp. 411–425.

Elliott, J. (2001) 'Making evidence-based practice educational', *British Educational Research Journal*, 27 (5) pp. 555–574.

Fenwick, T. (2014) 'Sociomateriality in medical practice and learning: attuning to what matters', *Medical Education* 48 (1) pp. 44–52.

Greany, T., Gu, Q., Handscomb, G. and Varley, M. (2014) *School-university partnerships: fulfilling the potential.* Bristol: National Coordinating Centre for Public Engagement.

Handscomb, G., Gu, Q. and Varley, M. (2014) *School-university partnerships: fulfilling the potential – literature review.* Bristol: National Coordinating Centre for Public Engagement.

Hargreaves, D. (1996) *Teaching as a research-based profession: possibilities and prospects.* London: TTA. Retrieved from: www.bit.ly/3bW4BgW [Accessed 4 October 2019].

Hillage, J., Pearson, R., Anderson, A. and Tamkin, P. (1998) *Excellence in research on schools.* Research report No. 74, Department for Education and Employment. London: The Stationery Office.

Jensen, K., Lahn, L. C. and Nerland, M. (eds) (2012) *Professional learning in the knowledge society.* Leiden: Brill.

Kushner, S., Simons, H., James, D., Jones, K and Yee, W. C. (2001) *TTA school based research consortia initiative: the evaluation – final report.* Bristol: University of the West of England.

McLaughlin, C., Cordingley, P., McLellan, R. and Baumfield, V. (2015) *Making a difference: turning teacher learning inside out.* Cambridge: Cambridge University Press.

Muijs, D. and Reynolds, D. (2002) 'Being or doing: the role of teacher behaviours and beliefs in school and teacher effectiveness in mathematics, a SEM analysis', *Journal of Classroom Interaction* 37 (2) pp. 3–15.

OECD (2003) *Knowledge management: new challenges for educational research.* Paris: OECD.

Stenhouse, L. (1975) *An introduction to curriculum research and development.* London: Heinemann.

TTA (1996) *Teaching as a research-based profession: promoting excellence in teaching.* London: TTA.

Tooley, J. and Darby, D. (1998) *Educational research: a critique.* London: Ofsted.

Zeichner, K., Payne, K. A. and Brayko, K. (2015) 'Democratising teacher education', *Journal of Teacher Education* 66 (2) pp. 122–135.

THE DIAMOND IN THE MINE

JONATHAN HASLAM *(@Jonathan_Haslam)*

Jonathan Haslam is the Director of the Institute for Effective Education and has been working for the last ten years to help practitioners and policy makers use research evidence in practice. He is the editor of *Best Evidence in Brief,* the IEE's e-newsletter, which is published each fortnight and goes to more than 5000 subscribers in the UK, with nearly 15,000 subscribers in the US and editions in Spanish and Chinese. He has been involved in a wide range of projects supporting evidence use, including the Research Schools Network and Evidence for the Frontline.

> *And there are no letters in the mailbox*
> *And there are no grapes upon the vine*
> *And there are no chocolates in the boxes anymore*
> *And there are no diamonds in the mine*
> *Leonard Cohen*

It's been a privilege to work on evidence-based reform over the last ten years. To watch as the landscape has changed, more robust research has been carried out, and interest in using that research has grown. But it has been exhausting. The intellectual and emotional effort that I have put in has been more than anything I have done previously. Ten years of struggling to understand the intersecting fields of research and practice. So where are we now? I think we're at an important stage in the movement, and perhaps equally at risk of falling back as moving forward. The risks come mostly, I think, from the danger that evidence-based reform won't deliver the results that people expect. More on this later; but first, let's go back ten years.

When I first began working on evidence-based reform in education, it seemed that here was a place where I could make a difference. If we could get the research evidence down from the library shelves, simplify it into words of less than six syllables, and get it out to teachers and schools, we could improve outcomes for children. It seemed like a substantial prize.

It has taken me a long time to figure out all the different elements, or building blocks, of evidence-based reform. And as I have tackled each in turn, I have come to see that there are challenges and limitations to each of them. Taken together, they are so substantial that I think we need to be clearer about what evidence-based reform can and can't deliver, so that practitioners are clear about what they are getting themselves into. I'm still a believer in evidence-based reform because the alternatives are worse; but we need to move to a situation where there is a better understanding of the challenges. The fact that so many careers in the sector rely on promising schools and practitioners the moon on a stick makes this difficult. A consultancy promising to make things a little bit better (probably, if you work hard at it) may not be the best business model, but it's the truth.

So what are the challenges?

THE STATE OF THE EVIDENCE

There is an awful lot of research evidence out there. But there is also a lot of awful research evidence out there. The awful research evidence tends to exaggerate the potential impact of new approaches and innovations. As a general rule of thumb, the better the research, the smaller the impact it claims. When we are looking for research to include in our *Best Evidence in Brief* newsletter,[1] if we find, for example, a meta-analysis that shows a large effect size, that is a red flag. The large effect has usually come about because the meta-analysis includes poor quality studies (e.g. of a short duration, researcher-designed measures, etc.). These kinds of

---

1. www.beib.org.uk

studies are unhelpful not just because they're not very good, but because they raise the expectations of the degree of change that we might see in the classroom. John Hattie's notion that only interventions with an effect size over +0.40 are educationally important is unhelpful. To set my stall out early, I think it is reasonable to expect that if you implemented the currently available best evidence across all aspects of school practice, you would see an average improvement of +0.30, maybe +0.40 if you're lucky. This is well worth having, but it doesn't, for example, quite close the achievement gap between disadvantaged students and their peers.

We don't have enough good evidence to rely upon. For example, the ratings for around 40% of the strategies listed in the EEF *Toolkit* are based on limited evidence or worse (including important issues such as performance pay and setting or streaming). So we can't yet be confident about the conclusions of this research. It may be that in the future, new studies overturn the current recommendations. In a way this is great: it's the progression of science and learning. It is important that we all stay curious. But this is an uncomfortable situation to be in for practice. Practitioners want a 'right answer' – should we stream or not? So equivocation on the evidence isn't very helpful, even if it's true.

Most interventions are no better than business as usual. Of 100 randomised controlled trials conducted by the Education Endowment Foundation, around one in five has evidence of a positive impact (Lortie-Forgues, 2019). This is something of a shock to the system. One of the objections to randomised controlled trials (RCTs) in education has been that it is unethical to deny the children in the control group the 'treatment' because there is an expectation that this shiny new approach will work. Now we find that almost the opposite is the case. It is much more likely that the treatment will not work (although thankfully it also usually causes no harm). In addition, although the EEF have conducted more than 100 RCTs, that still isn't enough useful evidence. We publish a website called *Evidence 4 Impact*,[2] which collects information on the interventions available to schools in England. The idea is that if schools are considering an intervention, they should look for one that has

2. www.evidence4impact.org.uk

evidence of effectiveness. We publish details on the intervention and any evidence of its effectiveness. Of the 171 interventions on the site, 16% have evidence of impact, 11% have been evaluated but showed no evidence of impact, and 73% have not been evaluated.

What does the fact that most interventions have no positive impact mean for the new ideas and initiatives that teachers and schools are trying every day in classrooms – not as part of a research project, but as part of everyday practice – up and down the country? Most new ideas come not from research but from colleagues in your own and nearby schools. Are they having any positive impact? The short answer is that we don't know. My view is that good teachers can make just about anything work if they think it's a good idea, and trying to improve your individual practice is a good thing. At the very least, it keeps you interested, enthusiastic, engaged, and it probably does no harm. But there isn't great evidence that teachers are continuously improving on their own. So small changes that are being introduced probably aren't making much difference, and are unlikely to be a source of undiscovered diamonds. But I'll come back to this later.

THE IMPACT OF TEACHERS AND SCHOOLS

The greatest influence on a student's achievement is the student themselves. Next in importance are their peers in the school. The impact of school itself comes in a distant third (Coleman et al., 1966; Gorard and Siddiqui, 2019). Within school, in each class, the effectiveness and therefore impact of an individual teacher is important, but it is proving difficult to identify effective teachers and improve less effective ones (the Gates Foundation spent $575 million in the US trying to do this, with no impact) (Stecher et al., 2018).

This noise in the system makes it difficult for teachers and schools to identify the impact of changes in school practice. Changes in the composition of the school (in classes and cohorts) can change outcomes in much more dramatic ways than those resulting from improving teaching and learning. It also makes it difficult to identify 'better' schools. Schools may be 'better' simply because their current student body is 'better' (regardless of attempts to level the demographic playing field, none of which are perfect). Visiting 'better' schools to identify their successful strategies isn't a bad idea, but it can be difficult to ascertain whether their success is actually due to those strategies, what those strategies are, and whether you can implement them in your own school.

Within a school, or a small group of schools, it can be difficult to identify the impact of new approaches. The IEE has now supported nearly 30 small-scale evaluations run by schools. The main learning point for the schools running these evaluations has probably been how difficult it is to organise a fair test within a school. The constraints of school organisation (timetabling, teacher-class allocation, curriculum structure, etc.) make it difficult for schools to isolate and evaluate the impact of a single change in practice. Yet such evaluation is essential. For, although it's not generalizable and may exaggerate the impact of the intervention (as small-scale studies tend to do), it's an important first indicator of whether the intervention should be scaled up or scaled back. Often, too, it provides useful information on the implementation of change across the school (for example, the extent to which other teachers can take up your idea effectively).

EVIDENCE-BASED REFORM

What do these challenges mean for the hopes of delivering evidence-based reform across the school system?

The evidence-based interventions available to schools are mostly built around practices with evidence of effectiveness – interventions to improve students' reading or maths skills, social-emotional learning, classroom talk, and so on. And, as we have seen, only a small proportion of those interventions have been shown to be positive.

Schools or practitioners can, of course, implement by themselves approaches that are supported by the evidence, though all the evidence suggests that this is challenging. Simply defining what the approach is can be surprisingly difficult. The EEF *Toolkit* has feedback as its top-rated strategy, but using feedback correctly is difficult. Dylan Wiliam identifies that, of eight ways to deliver feedback, only two result in a positive outcome (Wiliam, 2013).

The EEF's implementation guide advises that schools should specify the active ingredients of the intervention clearly: know where to be 'tight' and where to be 'loose'; and 'make thoughtful adaptations only when the active ingredients are securely understood and implemented' (Sharples et al., 2018). The problem with this advice is that the active ingredients or core components of an intervention are rarely, if ever, available to schools and practitioners. They are not included in EEF evaluation reports, or indeed information from most other education trials, even for something as critical as phonics. It is a nice idea, but one that currently does not work in practice, even assuming teachers have the research literacy skills, or perhaps research implementation skills, to do this.

It's also difficult for practitioners and schools to go directly to the research and try to implement research-proven strategies from there. Numerous EEF-supported pilots and trials have attempted this (Anglican Schools Partnership Effective Feedback, Hampshire Hundreds, Lesson Study, Research Champions, Research into Practice – Evidence-informed CPD in Rochdale, Research Learning Communities, and The Literacy Octopus) with no impact (Gorard et al., 2014; McNally, 2014; Murphy et al., 2017; Griggs et al., 2016; Speight et al., 2016, Rose et al., 2017; Lord et al., 2019). The RISE Project had a small impact, so although it wasn't statistically significant, it was perhaps the nearest to success (Wiggins et al., 2019). The lessons from the RISE Project suggest that school-wide, evidence-based improvement requires intensive training and coaching – arguably more intensive than anything we have seen to date. For schools, finding the resources to achieve this is going to be challenging. It requires extensive time (and therefore money) for staff to engage with training and development. It will also most likely require extensive input from external trainers and researchers, leading to further costs.

There are a few schools and school organisations trying to do this, and they make for interesting case studies (such as the Aspirer Teaching Alliance), where teachers are 'drenched' in opportunities to engage with the evidence (Dixon, 2019) but it's yet to be shown robustly (no matter how much I love them) the extent to which these schools can improve outcomes for themselves and, perhaps more importantly, for others. A whole-school improvement programme which has at its heart a school using research evidence to support school improvement does not yet exist. That is a missing piece in the puzzle, and only when we have that piece will we find out if such an approach is effective and what impact it might have. (How this might be developed is a whole other chapter – or possibly a book – on its own.)

Whole-school improvement programmes that are based on the best evidence do exist. One such, Success for All, has been evaluated in more than 20 trials and has shown an average effect size of +0.29. This gives an idea of the amount of improvement that evidence-based reform can deliver. It would be enough to close perhaps 50–75% of the gap between disadvantaged students and their peers (although the peers would also improve). Put another way, it would ensure that many more disadvantaged and previously lower-attaining students had the reading and maths skills to help them access the future curriculum and then succeed beyond school. A future whole-school improvement programme where the school uses research evidence itself might achieve more or less than this, but this is the area of impact we can expect.

This level of impact is only possible with intensive, whole-school implementation of evidence-based reform. Less intensive implementation than this will clearly have much less impact. So, for example, introducing metacognitive strategies across school or using retrieval practice starters is likely to have much less impact – impact that may be almost undetectable. What kind of impact are teachers and schools expecting from introducing such approaches, and how will they know if they have achieved it? The evaluation projects that we have supported have shown that this evaluation can be done, but it is not easy, or commonly carried out at the moment. It is more likely that teachers and schools will rely on the existing approaches they have to evaluate change. This may be fine, but as with the implementation of many new approaches in schools (the social-emotional aspects of learning (SEAL) programme comes to mind (Humphrey et al., 2010)) it is likely to result in a mix of beliefs about the effectiveness, from enthusiastic evangelist to disappointed sceptic. And here lies the risk: that evidence-based reform might end up being treated like any other fashion within schools – embraced or dismissed based on belief rather than science.

I think there are a number of issues that need further discussion and communication in order to ameliorate this risk:

- The potential impact that evidence-based reform can have within the school system. Let us all be clear about how much change can actually be achieved. How is this then presented to the wider community of parents and public? Can we agree a culture of realistic expectations?
- The effort that is required, from teachers and schools, to achieve this impact. Achieving the most impact requires relentless effort, but how should we balance this with the workload, mental health, recruitment and retention challenges that schools face?
- More and better evaluation of the impact that changes to practice are having (whether at a small-scale in-school level or all the way up to continuing randomised controlled trials), particularly of the interventions that schools are actually using.
- And, as in any research-based article, more research, particularly on issues that are important to schools, but under-researched.

I still believe that evidence-based reform is the best way of achieving significant, worthwhile improvement in outcomes for children, but I think it is vital that we have a shared understanding of how difficult these gains are to achieve, in order to avoid disappointment and disillusion with the evidence-based movement.

TOP TIPS FOR PRACTITIONERS

- It seems likely that sustained, school-wide engagement with research evidence is required to make a significant difference to pupil outcomes.
- For individual practitioners, though, there is still much benefit to be had from engaging with the research evidence, providing a rich source of ideas and challenge.

- Interest in research engagement has never been higher, and there is a vibrant, supportive community out there from whom you can benefit – distilling, reflecting, and applying research in practice.

REFERENCES

Coleman, J., Campbell, E., Hobson, C., McPartland, J., Mood, A., Weinfield, F. and York, R. (1966) *Equality of educational opportunity.* Washington, DC: US Department of Education and Welfare.

Dixon, M. (2019) Personal communication with Jonathan Haslam, 14 October.

Gorard, S. and Siddiqui, N. (2019) 'How trajectories of disadvantage help explain school attainment', *SAGE Open* 9 (1) pp. 1–14.

Gorard, S., See, B. H. and Siddiqui, N. (2014) *Anglican Schools Partnership: effective feedback – evaluation report and executive summary.* London: Education Endowment Foundation.

Griggs, J., Speight, S. and Farias, J. (2016) *Ashford Teaching Alliance Research Champion – evaluation report and executive summary.* London: Education Endowment Foundation.

Humphrey, N., Lendrum, A. and Wigelsworth, M. (2010) *Social and emotional aspects of learning programme in secondary schools: national evaluation.* Department for Education. London: The Stationery Office.

Lord, P., Rabiasz, A., Styles, B. and Andrade, J. (2019) 'Literacy Octopus' *dissemination trial – evaluation report and executive summary (addendum report).* London: Education Endowment Foundation.

Lortie-Forgues, H., Inglis, M. (2019) 'Rigorous large-scale educational RCTs are often uninformative: should we be concerned?', *Educational Researcher* 48 (3) pp. 158–166.

McNally, S. (2014) *Hampshire hundreds – evaluation report and executive summary.* London: Education Endowment Foundation.

Murphy, R., Weinhardt, F., Wyness, G. and Rolfe, H. (2017) *Lesson study – evaluation report and executive summary.* London: Education Endowment Foundation.

Rose, J., Thomas, S., Zhang, L., Edwards, A., Augero, A. and Roney, P. (2017) *Research learning communities – evaluation report and executive summary.* London: Education Endowment Foundation.

Sharples, J., Albers, B., Fraser, S. and Kime, S. (2018) *Putting evidence to work: a school's guide to implementation.* London: Education Endowment Foundation.

Speight, S., Callanan, M., Griggs, J. and Farias, J. (2016) *Rochdale research into practice – evaluation report and executive summary.* London: Education Endowment Foundation.

Stecher, B. M., Holtzman, D. J., Garet, M. S., Hamilton, L. S., Engberg, J., Steiner, E. D., Robyn, A., Baird, M. D., Gutierrez, I. A., Peet, E. D., Brodziak, I., Fronberg, K., Weinberger, G., Hunter, G. P. and Chambers, J. (2018) *Improving teaching effectiveness: final report.* Santa Monica, CA: RAND Corporation.

Wiggins, M., Jerrim, J., Tripney, J., Khatwa, M. and Gough, D. (2019) *The RISE project: evidence-informed school improvement.* London: Education Endowment Foundation.

Wiliam, D. (2013) *Embedding formative assessment with teacher learning communities* [Seminar slides]. Retrieved from: www.bit.ly/2HePEIA [Accessed 10 November 2019].

WHO JUDGES THE EVIDENCE FOR EVIDENCE-LED TEACHING?

STEPHEN GORARD (@SGorard)

Stephen Gorard is Professor of Education and Public Policy and Director of the Evidence Centre for Education at Durham University. He is a Fellow of the Academy of Social Sciences, member of the British Academy grants panel, and Lead Editor for *Review of Education*. His work concerns the robust evaluation of education as a lifelong process, focused on issues of equity, especially regarding school intakes. He is currently funded by the British Academy to investigate the impact of not attending school in India and Pakistan, and by Nesta to create a testbed for 12 edtech products for use in schools.

THE KEY PROBLEMS FOR EVIDENCE-LED TEACHING

It is clear that robust research evidence, adjusted to a local school or area context and combined with professional teacher judgements about priorities, should lead to a better education system. This, in turn, should help each new cohort of students to gain more from their schooling.

Happily, relevant robust research evidence in education exists, and is increasing as a body. But unhappily, the model of evidence use outlined above faces several immediate challenges. It is reasonable to expect teachers and school leads to be aware of context and to be able to judge what their improvement priorities are. But how can they judge which of all possible evidence is relevant, let alone judge how robust that evidence is?

Multiple systematic reviews of education research, in which all of the published and unpublished work on any topic is sought and then synthesised, have revealed that much of what is described as being 'research' is nothing of the sort. In addition, many reports of apparent research are indecipherable even to other professional researchers, and most of the remaining clearer reports portray research that is fundamentally flawed and should not be trusted or acted upon. There *are* good studies and, if found among the rest, they can be aggregated to begin to provide a basis for evidence-led teaching. However, this raises the question of who makes the quite complex judgements about which studies can be trusted, how their evidence is aggregated fairly, and how the synthetic results are best conveyed to their intended real-life users.

At one extreme, researchers could simply publish their research findings and make them available to teachers and other practitioners. Teachers would then have to judge for themselves which individual studies are relevant to their priority concern(s), how much to trust each study, and then how to aggregate the results of all relevant studies in an unbiased way. This is probably impractical, because teachers do not generally have the time or perhaps the skills needed to undertake such an enormous task.

At another extreme, the government could employ civil servants and others to find and sift the research studies, and then engineer them into a policy or legal framework requiring schools and teachers to act in accord with the ensuing evidence summary. Evidence use would be 'nationalised' and schools simply instructed how best to teach on the basis of best evidence. Experience suggests that this could well lead to the government taking into account factors that were not related to the evidence, and so come to biased and even ineffective or harmful recommendations. Governments may have the time and resource to undertake the task but currently do not have the skills needed to do so any more than most teachers do.

In between these two extremes lie a number of other plausible alternatives. Most, however, suffer from the same potential defect. Like the government idea, they require another link in the chain – a conduit between the research process and the use of research in schools. This leads back to the same question of who or what the conduit is that can be trusted to do the job and produce the best results.

In the US, UK and increasingly elsewhere, there are already a number of bodies set up to aggregate and simplify research results for real-life use. These include the What Works Centres and the Campbell Collaboration, and the task is also part of the remit of the Institute of Education Sciences and the Education Endowment Foundation. In the UK, there are plans by the Royal Society and British Academy (2018) to establish an Office for Educational Research that would presumably try to sort out all of this, as happened with the National Institute for Health and Care Excellence (NICE) for healthcare in the UK (Perry et al., 2010). As suggested by the evidence summary later in this chapter, this is not a solution in itself.

Another possibility is that the likely users of research conduct, or at least help run, the research themselves. This might lead to an increased uptake, and 'ownership', of the findings, but this may also not be practical. Looking at what we already know is a key part of preparing to conduct new research (Gorard, 2013), but teachers are unlikely to be able to do this first step (as discussed above). It is even more unlikely that teachers can complete such a review of existing evidence and then conduct their own studies and interpret the results securely. There is no real reason to believe that this approach is a solution in itself either.

Another distinct problem, therefore, is that despite a slow growth over 20 years in the number of high-quality studies of education, there has been no equivalent increase in the robust research on how to get the evidence from those high-quality studies into widespread use amongst teachers.

WHAT DOES THE EXISTING EVIDENCE SAY?

The results of a large-scale review of the published and unpublished literature on how best to get research evidence into use is described in full in Gorard et al. (2019). We found 323 relevant studies across all areas of public policy – including health, housing and social work – and judged them in terms of quality. Very few (33) were of an appropriate design for making causal claims about evidence-into-use, and even fewer were about education. There is little robust causal evidence on the types of intervention that actually encourage teachers to take account of research in their decision making. Most studies do not even assess whether practice changes after dissemination, let alone whether student (or patient) results improve as a consequence. Generally, research on practitioners' uptake of evidence is based on self-reports and interviews. It is shocking how much of the research into evidence use is not itself robustly evidence-informed.

Passive approaches

It is clear, though, that simply making evidence available to users is not an appropriate method of general transfer, and this is the case whether access consists of full open access to research articles or a research summary or toolkit wherein the results are combined and modified. These essenNo. Leave tially passive approaches reach only a subset of their intended audiences and do not promote regular or sustained use of evidence. Many such summaries are also being increasingly criticised for their bias or an overly casual approach to quality control.

These conclusions do not change depending on the format used to present the research findings or summaries. In fact, with a passive approach to transfer, simply modifying research findings into easier formats may not lead to any better results than access to full articles (Bero et al., 1998). Comparing a scientific summary, a plain language summary and a visual representation as ways of presenting knowledge about the results of Cochrane systematic reviews in health, practitioners, students and the public all preferred the visual representation (Buljan et al., 2017). However, the infographic was shown to be no better for actually imparting knowledge of the findings. In healthcare, merely disseminating best practice guidelines is insufficient to alter practice in most cases (Gonzales et al., 2012). Systematic syntheses of evidence, it would seem, have little impact on practice without further translation and activity (Haines et al., 2004; Green et al., 2016).

More active approaches

Practitioners usually claim that bespoke training or workshops in understanding evidence (whether generically or on a specific programme) do help them to understand it better, and therefore to use it appropriately. However, training and dissemination workshops often have poor attendance after initial enthusiasm (Dagenais et al., 2013). Comparing a half-day critical appraisal skills training workshop with a control, Taylor et al. (2004) found that the ability to appraise evidence in a systematic review was higher in the workshop group, but there was no difference in the attitude towards using evidence, and no evidence of subsequent changes in practice or behaviour. Similar results appear in a review of the impact of practitioner workshops on use of health evidence (Gülmezoglu et al., 2007), and from a review of nine randomised control trials comparing lectures, online delivery, small group work, and directed or self-directed learning (Ilic and Maloney, 2014). None stood out as any better at getting evidence into use. This is part of the reason why there is no value in simply asking stakeholders what they think works in getting evidence into use.

The Literacy Octopus trials evaluated the impact of providing teachers in a total of 13,323 schools with research summaries and evidence-based resources to improve teaching, with or without light-touch support (NFER 2017). After two years, there was little or no increase in any of six measures of teachers' use of research, and no improvement in pupils' key stage 2 English scores compared with the control group. The additional support made no difference either way.

There is no evidence yet that just linking users and researchers in research projects, perhaps via user groups as encouraged by research funders, is effective (McLean et al., 2018). Two-way secondments between government and research departments are feasible, but, like so many others, this approach has not been tested directly, and is only considered via surveys and similar (Uneke et al., 2018). So although these more active approaches are reported as preferred by users, they do not seem to make any actual difference in practice.

Schools having research leads or champions to interpret and collate relevant evidence for them is a slightly more promising approach, and led to small positive effect sizes in one UK study (Wiggins et al., 2019). However, there was a high turnover of leads, as noted in other studies (Rose et al., 2017). Research leads have been reported to make no difference to student attainment (Griggs et al., 2016), or future teacher behaviour (Speight et al. 2016). The University of Bristol (2017) evaluated the use of the *Research Learning Communities* project, in which experts discussed research evidence with evidence champions from 60 intervention schools. This study of 5462 pupils showed no improvement in test outcomes compared to 59 control schools after two years.

Ongoing active approaches
Active approaches seem to need ongoing monitoring and auditing to confirm that evidence is being used, and is being implemented properly. This moves us closer to a government-mandated and enforced procedure for evidence use.

Individual coaching on evidence-informed approaches for specific topics, with individual feedback, is perhaps the most promising approach (Miller et al., 2006), although an evaluation of a dental hygiene intervention based in 20 cities, with 385 registered hygienists randomised to intervention and 366 to control, suggests that self-study can be almost as effective and is, of course, cheaper to implement (Gordon et al., 2005). Some 'training' interventions based on small group workshops and follow-ups have shown that knowledge among health practitioners increased at post-test, but there are no differences in treatment behaviour or patient outcomes, according to a trial of medical practitioners (Forsetlund et al., 2003). Similarly using communities of practice with software follow-up was linked via a trial of mental health practitioners to having greater knowledge of a mental health intervention, but not to reporting greater readiness to change practice, or reporting actual change of practice (Barwick et al., 2009). This is all rather depressing for evidence into use.

According to a review of 12 interventions by Menon et al. (2009), interactive multi-component interventions can improve health practitioner knowledge of evidence, and the practitioners can then change their practice behaviour, compared to passive dissemination of evidence. A prolonged audit and feedback intervention was effective at persuading dentists to undertake antibiotic prescribing in line with the current evidence (Elouafkaoui et al., 2016). There is further evidence from a systematic review of healthcare interventions that audit and feedback is the most effective way to get evidence into use, at least for the short term and often combined with other approaches (Siddiqi et al. 2005), although some studies find the combination only moderately effective (Davis and Taylor-Vaisey, 1997). It is also not yet clear how this could be translated to teaching practice.

These more active approaches show more promise than those simply considering how evidence should be presented. The strongest evidence does suggest that both user knowledge and user behaviour can be made more evidence-led with active presentation and then auditing/monitoring. The situation for improved student attainment or similar end-user outcomes is less clear, largely because there is so little work on this.

Legislation and enforced use of evidence

The final approach considered here is the enforced use of evidence by policy-makers and practitioners. Kansagra and Farley (2011) draw a distinction between evidence-based interventions in health that are implemented at an individual level and those implemented at a population level. The former would inlcude the prescription of metformin for those diagnosed with diabetes, which is a treatment that requires initial and continuing actions by the patient. An example of the latter is the fluoridation of water to prevent dental caries. The latter have a lower cost per individual treated, and are more reliable than individual treatments. Such an intervention has to be so heavily engineered that its evidence base is no longer clear to the user. A practice example would be clinical guidelines for nurses (Thomson et al., 2000). In nursing, there is a requirement for all clinical practice policies and procedures to be evidence-based (Oman et al., 2008). Such an approach has been enforced in health settings via the use of report cards (Valentine et al., 2014). It is likely that if evidence is to improve education successfully then more of such enforced or population-level measures need to be developed, validated, and implemented.

To be eligible for federal school improvement funding under the US Every Student Succeeds Act, schools must use one of the top three categories of programmes – based on evidence-based interventions (California Department of Education, n.d.). Similarly, the US Department of Education Investing in Innovation (i3) programme provided large grants for applicants wanting to improve attainment at their schools (www.bit.ly/2vrv3hO). The largest grants required applicants to use interventions rated as effective by the What Works Clearinghouse.

Successful UK REF case studies in education suggest that the underpinning research with real-life impact is usually invisible to teachers, and is instead embedded in artefacts such as services and technologies, pre-prepared lesson plans and resources (Cain and Allan, 2017).

However, these approaches have not been clearly evaluated (Longjohn and Vojta, 2012), although see Doabler et al. (2014). While enforced/population use of evidence-led approaches is probably the most effective way to get evidence-into-use, considerably more research would be needed to decide that.

CONCLUSIONS – THE CORE OF THE PROBLEM

A total of 33 studies (or reviews that include such studies), relevant to getting evidence into use, were found in the review. There was no space to mention them all here, but those left out do not alter the main conclusions. Most were in health or fields other than education. This means that much of the improved evidence in education generated in the past 20 years could have been wasted or at least not used most effectively because we have so little idea how to put evidence into use. Users do not usually act in accordance with evidence (Epstein, 2017). The findings of high-quality substantive research have not become embedded in practice, while too much lower-quality evidence is still being actively promoted by developers, researchers and funders. This is a huge problem.

Providing access to research evidence, whether simplified or not, is not generally an effective way of getting it used. Nor does it make much difference if that evidence is presented to users by knowledge-brokers, in short courses or similar. What is more likely to work for both policy and practice is identifying high-quality evidence, engineering it fairly into a more usable format, and presenting it actively or iteratively. We need trusted conduits to do this job (trusted to do it without fear or favour).

TOP TIPS

- As educators we need to agree quickly on some basic standards for education research so that the task of sifting is made easier by losing much of the research that is just a waste of time and money in the future.
- Funders need to stop funding research that is nowhere near trustworthy, and to build up libraries of successfully tested programmes.
- Teachers need to overcome any resistance to using and learning about research, so that they do not simply have research-led approaches imposed upon them.

REFERENCES

Barwick, M., Peters, J. and Boydell, K. (2009) 'Getting to uptake: do communities of practice support the implementation of evidence-based practice?', *Journal of the Canadian Academy of Child and Adolescent Psychiatry* 18 (1) pp. 16–29.

Bero, L. A., Grilli, R., Grimshaw, J. M., Harvey, E., Oxman, A. D. and Thomson, M. A. (1998) 'Closing the gap between research and practice: an overview of systematic reviews of interventions to promote the implementation of research findings', *The BMJ (Clinical Research Ed.)* 317 (7156) pp. 465–468.

Buljan, I., Malički, M., Wager, E., Puljak, L., Hren, D., Kellie, F., West, H., Alfirević, Z. and Marušić, A. (2017) 'No difference in knowledge obtained from infographic or plain language summary of a Cochrane systematic review: three randomized controlled trials', *Journal of Clinical Epidemiology* 97 (1) pp. 86–94. Retrieved from: www.bit.ly/2vq1qNE [Accessed 3 October 2019].

Cain, T. and Allan, D. (2017) 'The invisible impact of educational research', *Oxford Review of Education* 43 (6) pp. 718–732.

California Department of Education (n.d.) *Evidence-based interventions under the ESSA*. Retrieved from: www.bit.ly/2UKTSjl [Accessed 3 October 2019].

Dagenais, C., Queuille, L. and Ridde, V. (2013) 'Evaluation of a knowledge transfer strategy from a user fee exemption program for vulnerable populations in Burkina Faso', *Global Health Promotion* 20 (1 suppl) pp. 70–79.

Davis, D. and Taylor-Vaisey, A. (1997) 'Translating guidelines into practice: a systematic review of theoretic concepts, practical experience and research evidence in the adoption of clinical practice guidelines', *Canadian Medical Association Journal* 157 (4) pp. 408–416.

Doabler, C., Nelson, N., Kosty, D., Fien, H., Baker, S., Smolkowski, K., and Clark, B. (2014) 'Examining teachers' use of evidence-based practices during core mathematics instruction', *Assessment for Effective Intervention* 39 (2) pp. 99–111.

Elouafkaoui, P., Young, L., Newlands, R., Duncan, E. M., Elders, A., Clarkson, J. E. and Ramsay, C. R. (2016) 'An audit and feedback intervention for reducing antibiotic prescribing in general dental practice', *PLOS Medicine* 13 (8).

Epstein, D. (2017) 'When evidence says no, but doctors say yes', *The Atlantic* [Online], 22 February. Retrieved from: www.bit.ly/2w5VbPm [Accessed 8 October 2019].

Forsetlund, L., Talseth, K., Bradley, P., Nordheim, L. and Bjorndal, A. (2003) 'Many a slip between cup and lip. Process evaluation of a program to promote and support evidence-based public health practice', *Evaluation Review* 27 (2) pp. 179–209.

Gonzales, R., Handley, M., Ackerman, S. and O'Sullivan, P. (2012) 'Increasing the translation of evidence into practice, policy, and public health improvements', *Academic Medicine* 87 (3) pp. 271–278.

Gorard, S. (2013) *Research design: creating robust approaches for the social sciences.* London: SAGE.

Gorard, S., Griffin, N., See, B. H. and Siddiqui, N. (2019) *How can we get educators to use research evidence?* Raleigh, NC: Lulu Press.

Gordon, J. S., Andrews, J. A., Lichtenstein, E., Severson, H. H. and Akers, L. (2005) 'Disseminating a smokeless tobacco cessation intervention model to dental hygienists: a randomized comparison of personalized instruction and self-study methods', *Health Psychology* 24 (5) pp. 447–455.

Green, C., Taylor, C., Buckley, S. and Hean, S. (2016) 'Beyond synthesis: augmenting systematic review procedures with practical principles to optimise impact and uptake in educational policy and practice', *International Journal of Research and Method in Education* 39 (3) pp. 329–344.

Griggs, J., Speight, S. and Farias, J. (2016) *Ashford Teaching Alliance Research Champion – evaluation report and executive summary.* London: Education Endowment Foundation.

Gülmezoglu, A., Langer, A., Piaggio, G., Lumbiganon, P., Villar, J. and Grimshaw, J. (2007) 'Cluster randomized trial of an active, multifaceted information dissemination intervention based on the WHO reproductive health library to change obstetric practices', *BJOG* 114 (1) pp. 16–23.

Haines, A., Kuruvilla, S., and Borchert, M. (2004) 'Bridging the implementation gap between knowledge and action for health', *Bulletin of the World Health Organization* 82 (10) pp. 724–731.

Ilic, D. and Maloney, S. (2014) 'Methods of teaching medical trainees evidence-based medicine: a systematic review', *Medical Education* 48 (2) pp. 124–135.

Kansagra, S. and Farley, T. (2011) 'Public health research: lost in translation or speaking the wrong language?', *American Journal of Public Health* 101 (12) pp. 2203–2206.

Longjohn, M. and Vojta, D. (2012) 'Translating research into evidence-based practice', *American Journal of Public Health* 102 (8) p. e5.

McLean, R. K. D., Graham, I. D., Tetroe, J. M. and Volmink, J. A. (2018) 'Translating research into action: an international study of the role of research funders', *Health Research Policy and Systems* 16 (44).

Menon, A., Korner-Bitensky, N., Kastner, M., McKibbon, K. and Straus, S. (2009) 'Strategies for rehabilitation professionals to move evidence-based knowledge into practice: a systematic review', *Journal of Rehabilitation Medicine* 41 (13) pp. 1024–1032.

Miller, W., Sorensen, J., Selzer, J. and Brigham, G. (2006) 'Disseminating evidence-based practices in substance abuse treatment: a review with suggestions', *Journal of Substance Abuse Treatment* 31 (1) pp. 25–39.

NFER (2017) *The Literacy Octopus: communicating and engaging with research.* Retrieved from: www.bit.ly/2SWfGXJ [Accessed 8 October 2019].

Oman, K., Duran, C. and Fink, R. (2008) 'Evidence-based policy and procedures: an algorithm for success', *The Journal of Nursing Administration* 38 (1) pp. 47–51.

Perry, A., Amadeo, C., Fletcher, M. and Walker, E. (2010) *Instinct or reason: how education policy is made and how we might make it better.* Reading: Education Development Trust. Retrieved from: www.bit.ly/2SjzKD5 [Accessed 7 October 2019].

Rose, J., Thomas, S., Zhang, L., Edwards, A., Augero, A. and Roney, P. (2017) *Research learning communities – evaluation report and executive summary.* London: Education Endowment Foundation.

Royal Society and British Academy (2018) *Harnessing educational research.* Retrieved from: www.bit.ly/38LFfjK [Accessed 10 October 2019].

Siddiqi, K., Newell, J. and Robinson, M. (2005) 'Getting evidence into practice: what works in developing countries?', *International Journal for Quality in Health Care* 17 (5) pp. 447–454.

Speight, S., Callahan, M., Griggs, J. and Farias, J. C. (2016) *Rochdale research into practice – evaluation report and executive summary.* London: Education Endowment Foundation

Taylor, R., Reeves, B., Ewings, P. and Taylor, R. (2004) 'Critical appraisal skills training for health care professionals: a randomized controlled trial', *BMC Medical Education* 4, article number 30.

Thomson, P., Angus, N. and Scott, J. (2000) 'Building a framework for getting evidence into critical care education and practice', *Intensive and Critical Care Nursing* 16 (3) pp. 164–174.

Uneke, C., Ezeoha, A., Uro-Chukwu, H., Ezeonu, C. and Igboji, J. (2018) 'Promoting researchers and policy-makers collaboration in evidence-informed policy-making in Nigeria', *International Journal of Health Policy Management* 7 (6) pp. 522–531.

University of Bristol (2017) *Research learning communities.* Retrieved from: www.bit.ly/2SBK9Jn [Accessed 8 October 2019].

Valentine, A., DeAngelo, D., Alegría, M. and Cook, B. (2014) 'Translating disparities research to policy: a qualitative study of state mental health policymakers' perceptions of mental health care disparities report cards', *Psychological Services* 11 (4) pp. 377–387.

Wiggins, M., Jerrim, J., Tripney, J., Khatwa, M. and Gough, D. (2019) *The RISE project: evidence-informed school improvement.* London: Education Endowment Foundation.

TEACHER-INFORMED RESEARCH

KAREN WESPIESER *(@KarenWespieser)*

Karen is a social researcher and has worked in the education sector for 20 years. She is passionate about increasing and communicating the use of evidence in education to positively impact the lives of young people. Karen is also a school governor, trustee of education charity Parentkind, founder of #UKEdResChat, and a mum of two.

INTRODUCTION

Let's start with a confession. I am not a teacher. Apart from a short stint as a teaching assistant back in 1999, I have never been directly employed by a school. Despite this, I have spent nearly 20 years involved in designing research and policy that tries to help schools improve the outcomes for young people. Over this time, whilst the edu-support sector has grown, it seems to me that the distance between those in the classroom and those of us trying to help has increased exponentially.

In this chapter, I will outline some of the reasons why I think this gap has grown and how it can be narrowed.

FIELDWORK IS NOW THE EXCEPTION RATHER THAN THE NORM

In the early noughties, in my first job as a research assistant at one of the country's largest dedicated education research institutions, I spent most of my time zipping up and down the country visiting schools, interviewing those who work in them and collecting information from the chalk-face. Fast-forward 20 years and for most research projects I am involved with, fieldwork is now the exception rather than the norm. While there are a number of grassroots organisations encouraging teachers to become more engaged with research and policymakers, where are the organisations encouraging researchers and policymakers to engage with teachers?

One reason that fewer researchers visit schools is a ground-shift in methodologies over the past 20 years. Once, if you wanted to find out something about, say, teacher retention, you would need to conduct a large-scale survey and triangulate that data with case studies or interviews. Now there is the school workforce census: a tidy dataset that compiles a number of different school reporting functions and stretches back in its current iteration to 2010. The school workforce census provides a one-stop shop for researchers – or anyone else who's interested – with a clear picture of what is going on in terms of staffing in every school in England. The same is available for pupil-level data, funding data, and soon, destinations data, which, through database wizardry, is being analysed by combining data from DfE, HMRC and the DWP. So, with this amount of information, it is perhaps not necessary (and certainly not encouraged) to *bother* schools with research requests.

Another key change in the research landscape was the introduction of the Education Endowment Foundation (EEF) in 2011. Overnight, the EEF became the biggest funder of school research in England (*The Economist*, 2018). The scale of funding had an unprecedented influence over research methodologies. The EEF are unapologetic about their penchant for randomised control trials (RCTs) and meta-analysis (the combing of quantitative findings from studies which are not identical to provide more robust estimates). In just six years, the EEF more than doubled the amount of available evidence from trials in education in this country and boasts that it has commissioned more than 10% of all known trials in education around the world (ibid.). As with the big data created by the government's national datasets, EEF trial data is predominantly quantitative. Only around a third of RCTs include a process evaluation (Connolly et al., 2018) – the part of the research that gets into schools, speaks with teachers and leaders and attempts to understand *why* an effect observed in the data is happening.

Don't get me wrong: these quantitative methodologies are not bad in themselves. Far from it: they have allowed insights and developments the like of which we haven't seen before. The problem is that with finite research resources, studies using these methodologies are prioritised over other types of research; the types of education research where researchers and teachers meet can be considered along with context and culture.

Perhaps the biggest problem with these quantitative approaches, though, comes at the end of the research process. Researchers who have spent their careers in front of screens, interacting with binary values rather than real people, will find it very difficult to write a report that will change the behaviour of teachers that they have never met, or influence the outcomes of children that they have never seen. Take, for example, some of the best-known research into bullying (Farrington and Ttofi, 2009). The researchers examined the effectiveness of anti-bullying programmes and considered which intervention methods are most likely to reduce school bullying. To do this, they conducted a meta-analysis looking at more than 600 studies; but they did not meet with any teachers or pupils. Because of this ivory-tower approach, the recommendations from this really interesting research are targeted at policymakers and researchers. There are no suggestions about what those at the front line should do, even though you would imagine that 'improving the school playground environment through reorganisation and/or identification of bullying hot spots' would be easier for schools to do than policymakers!

The final barrier is that too often we can fool ourselves that researchers are already interacting with the school workforce. Admittedly not in real life, but online. Teacher bloggers and interest groups on Facebook and Twitter are lively fora for potential interactions between different stakeholders. But, what we need to remember is that only a minority of teachers are represented – guesstimates range at around 6%–10% – and that this minority are likely to be quite different to the majority of their colleagues (if nothing else, the considerable time some individuals put into their social media suggests a different type of engagement to their colleagues who prefer to use social media to keep up to date with family and friends). Compare the proportion of teachers who are using social media professionally with the proportion of journalists or MPs taking this approach and you will see that you have a minority talking to the majority – something it's all too easy to forget inside a social media bubble.

As with my critique of quantitative methodologies, I am not saying that engaging with teachers via social media is a bad thing; nor am I suggesting that we should criticise those that do. However, we do need to be aware that when high-profile bloggers or Twitterati are invited to represent the profession on research steering groups or DfE working groups, or are name-dropped by the Education Secretary, this isn't on a new relationship between teachers, researchers and policymakers, but simply a clique that has probably always been at the centre of our education system.

It is in keeping with the zeitgeist to claim to be a 'research-engaged teacher'. Where I think there is a growing gap is in the number of teacher-engaged researchers and policymakers. Big data, quantitative methodologies and social media have led to a situation where those seeking to support teachers no longer *need* to visit schools to do their jobs. Despite this, there are more reasons than ever that they *ought* to visit schools. Far from this being a burden on busy teachers working in those institutions, I truly believe that many would welcome these visitors with open arms.

HOW TO BE A TEACHER-ENGAGED RESEARCHER

If research methods no longer necessitate going into school on a regular basis, how else could these engagements take place? From a research perspective, it could include steering groups, advisory groups, or participatory workshops which bring together everyday teachers, school leaders and researchers. Practical inputs could be sought on the design of surveys or interview schedules, data interpretation, and perhaps most importantly, how to ensure that research reports include useful and timely recommendations for teachers and leaders. EEF guidance reports utilise this model and have resulted in a range of useful outputs, such as *Preparing For Literacy* (Education Endowment Foundation, 2018a), and *Metacognition And Self-regulated Learning* (Education Endowment Foundation, 2018b).

It needn't all be related to the day job either. A simple way to gain insight about day-to-day school life is through volunteering. This could be as a school governor or trustee. In exchange for sharing your unique experiences, perspectives and insights, you can gain significant insights into schools' challenges – and celebrations – and get a true feel for the cycle of the school year. Alternatively, you could join a student mentoring programme, or simply offer to sit and listen to children read.

Finally, make sure you engage outside of your echo chamber. A simple way to do this could be to follow hashtags and not just individuals. #UKEdResChat and #CogSciSci both bring teachers and researchers together in a constructive way, and you don't even need to join Twitter to read the interactions.

PERVERSE INCENTIVES

Witnessing the gap between practitoners and researchers is one of the reasons I started the #UKEdResChat Twitter events. The initial aim of the chat was to bridge the gap between researchers and teachers, but it became apparent very quickly that there were far more teachers participating than academics.

There are a number of regularly occurring themes in the chats. How can teachers access research? How can teachers find the time to read research? How can teachers interpret the quality of research?

The responses, predominantly provided by the teaching community on Twitter, frequently come from the research users and not the research creators. They suggest research mediators, synthesis created by third parties, a greater focus on research in initial teacher training.

But more can be done by the academic community and the incentives within it that create barriers to work with teachers. The Research Assessment Exercise (RAE) prioritises academic impact over practical impact: you get a higher 'score' for explaining your research to your academic peers than you do for explaining it to the people you are actually researching *for*. The language required by journals and doctoral study is, by definition, academic. But need it be academic to the point of excluding mainstream readers? Could plain English be used more frequently?

CONCLUSION

Of course, this chapter has been a generalisation of the issue. Just as there are some schools and some teachers who are more engaged with research than others, there are also researchers and research institutions that are more engaged with teachers than others. This book contains some wonderful examples of these collaborations, so I do not need to list them here. My call is simply for more!

Maybe we always view the past through rose-tinted glasses, and maybe it's simple nostalgia that makes me feel like there was a more authentic connection between researchers and the classroom in the past. But the teacher-led movement to engage in research should not be one-sided. Academics should never again be characterised as 'the blob'. Researchers need to step up and engage. This shift is essential if we want to narrow the gap between research and practice.

TOP TIPS

- Make use of steering or advisory groups to ensure there is a dialogue between researchers and teachers throughout the research process.
- Think of different ways that researchers can be present in schools – as governors, as mentors, as readers, as researchers-in-residence.
- Engage outside of your echo chamber by following hashtags on social media, not just individuals.

REFERENCES

Connolly, P., Keenan, C. and Urbanska, K. (2018) 'The trials of evidence-based practice in education: a systematic review of randomised controlled trials in education research 1980–2016', *Educational Research* 60 (3) pp. 276–291. Retrieved from: www.bit.ly/2uDTI2t [Accessed 7 November 2019].

The Economist (2018) 'England has become one of the world's biggest education laboratories', 31 March. Retrieved from: www.econ.st/3bpMvUa [Accessed 7 November 2019].

Education Endowment Foundation (2018a) *Preparing for literacy: improving communication, language and literacy in the early years.* London: Education Endowment Foundation. Retrieved from: www.bit.ly/2SCOVX9 [Accessed 7 November 2019].

Education Endowment Foundation (2018b) *Metacognition and self-regulated learning*. London: Education Endowment Foundation. Retrieved from: www. bit.ly/3byUf6f [Accessed 7 November 2019].

Farrington, D. P. and Ttofi, M. M. (2009) 'School-based programs to reduce bullying and victimization'. *Campbell Systematic Reviews* 5 (1) pp. i–148. Retrieved from: www.bit.ly/39Es6t5 [Accessed 7 November 2019].

¡VIVA LA REVOLUCIÓN!

CHRIS BROWN, JANE FLOOD & GRAHAM HANDSCOMB

In 2019, two of us (Chris Brown and Jane Flood) wrote a book for school leaders on how they could get the most from engaging in professional learning networks. The book was based on a small-scale research project, but our conclusions seemed to have the potential to stretch beyond the case in hand. Specifically, what we realised from our study was that if school leaders are to lead change in a meaningful way, they needed to focus on three things:

1. Formalising the change – ensuring the change in question remains a key focus across the school and that its importance is recognised by all stakeholders
2. Prioritising the change – ensuring appropriate support is available through the allocation of resources to enable the work associated with the change to be achieved
3. Mobilising the change – ensuring new knowledge and practice relating to, or emerging from, the change can be accessed and engaged with

We are privileged, along with our co-editor Graham Handscomb, to have been able to bring together a really talented group of practitioners, researchers and other key players to express their views on how to make the research-informed revolution a reality. But what has really struck us is how the themes from what people have been saying once again return to these three core needs. Bringing together insights from across the book, we feel that a number of key lessons emerge for making research use a reality in schools. In relation to formalising, prioritising and mobilising, these lessons are as follows.

WHAT WE HAVE LEARNED ABOUT FORMALISATION

It is vital that research-informed practice is formally linked to the policies and processes of the school. Making this link signals the importance of the work, and also that engaging in research is not 'just another initiative', but something that is key to a school's culture and way of working. Approaches to formalising research use encompass the inclusion of such activity in school improvement plans and teachers' performance management targets (making it clear that it is part of teachers' roles, e.g. as noted in Claire Harley's and Cat Scutt's chapters; also see the chapter by Maria Cunningham and David Weston). This, in turn, ensures that research engagement is on the radar of the school's governing body (e.g. see chapters by Hanna Miller and Karen Wespieser). At the same time, such signals need to be meaningful. There is no point adding priorities to a school improvement plan if there are already so many that the notion of something being a 'priority' no longer has currency. Other learning here includes the use of routines, such as learning sets (Lindsay Palmer), having in place the right supporting structures and tools (Graham Handscomb, Cat Scutt and Julie Nelson) and showing that taking reasonable risks in the pursuit of innovation is OK (Claire Harley).

WHAT WE HAVE LEARNED ABOUT PRIORITISATION

Ask any teacher around the world how they could best be supported to engage with a new initiative and, invariably, time will feature in their response. Teachers are overburdened and if we want them to do more of something, we need to ensure they can do less of something else (this is nicely espoused in Adam Boxer's chapter). This seems to be especially true for schools in challenging circumstances where some of the teachers often admit they are struggling simply to stay afloat. Often, school leaders have the freedom to change structures within their school to free up time. For example: by 'shaving' time from lessons to create a free half day once a week; by reallocating meeting time or preparation, planning and assessment time; or through smart approaches to timetabling (for instance, Marcella McCarthy's chapter explores the use of INSET days). Affording time to teachers will go a long way to helping them engage in research effectively, but time also needs to be allocated to help teachers engage with their colleagues to ensure the mobilisation of research can occur. This also means that processes within the school need to be used to facilitate research-related collaboration. For instance, timetables should reflect the need for collaboration between particular groups of teachers. Within prioritisation we also have suggestions from Sarah Seleznyov, Raphael Wilkins and Dom Wyse for building the capacity of teachers to engage effectively and critically with research; likewise, Gary Jones discusses ensuring how teachers can be supported to get behind the motivations of those producing research.

WHAT WE HAVE LEARNED ABOUT MOBILISATION

Mobilisation is complex and teachers and school leaders still have much to learn in this area. However, the work here has provided some vital clues as to how mobilisation can be improved. In particular, as well as enforcing the notion that passive dissemination is ineffectual (e.g. Stephen Gorard's chapter), it has shown that the most impactful forms of mobilisation involve school staff:

- actually engaging with innovations
- collaboratively testing out how new practices can be used to improve teaching and learning
- continuing to use and refine new practices in an ongoing way (this comes through from most of the chapters authored by teachers; also see Brown, 2019)

This is because supporting staff to actively engage and experiment with new practices helps them to develop as experts. In turn, this means that the use of research-informed innovations and practices will be both refined and sustained over time, allowing students to benefit from their ongoing improvement. In addition, it matters who is doing the mobilising. As was demonstrated by Sarah Seleznyov and others, research champions should ideally be chosen based on their position in school social networks, meaning they have the power, the access and the ability to influence whether and how innovations are adopted by others. Also key is ready access to research (which is nicely explored by Steve Higgins).

PURSUE DESIRABLE OUTCOMES

Adam Boxer's chapter reminds us that while it is possible to find effective ways to achieve almost any outcome, what we should also be doing is pursing outcomes that fit with our values. What we mean here can be illustrated by the criminal justice policies pursued by the New Labour government between 1997 and 2010 and the subsequent Conservative/ Liberal Democrat coalition government of 2010 to 2015. New Labour's policies were incredibly successful in reducing crime, with figures from the Crime Survey for England and Wales showing a decrease (excluding fraud and computer misuse) from 17 million offences in 1997 to 9.5 million offences in 2010. The approach taken by New Labour 'worked' because of both net-widening and the replacement of non-custodial sentencing with short-term sentences (of three to six months) for many less serious crimes. In other words, criminals were now being locked up and taken off the streets. Effective, yes; but in the longer term, the use of such sentences tended to have a negative impact on recidivism, the likelihood that criminals go on to commit crimes in the future.

All this changed in 2010, however, when the newly elected Conservative/Liberal Democrat coalition started to explore the possibilities of restorative justice for lesser crimes – an approach that has been shown to have a positive impact both on recidivism and for the victims of crime.[1] Restorative justice was seen by the coalition to be more desirable because, longer term, it meant there should be less crime, a more successful integration of criminals back into society and less

---

1. See www.bit.ly/38saiBd

victim trauma. Essentially the approaches pursued by New Labour and the coalition represent one research-informed approach versus another. Both 'worked' to meet their goals and could be regarded as effective. Choosing between the two really depended on both the values and the goals of the policymakers concerned, as well as the ideological window that framed their thinking.

Returning to education, and what this example illustrates is that while we can certainly find ways of operating successfully within current accountability structures (in other words, we can achieve research-informed short-term gains in the performance of our students), what we should ideally be doing is finding ways of being successful that fit both our values as teachers and the concerns of a wider group of stakeholders. For instance, the concerns of parents, the local community, employers and, of course, students themselves. To that end, we should be starting our research-informed journey by asking ourselves questions, such as: 'What difference do we want to make to our students' lives?' or 'What kind of future citizens do we want to help mould with our curriculum and pedagogy?' Our answers might include wanting students to be knowledgeable now, but we are likely to also want this knowledge to stick with them in the longer term once they have left our care. At the same time, we might also decide that we want to ensure students develop a thirst for learning and an understanding of how to learn that lasts them a lifetime. Asking these questions and reflecting on our responses is likely to open up a range of tensions that we have to find ways to overcome, since our short- and long-term aspirations may be in conflict both with each other and the more general constraints and demands we face in our roles. This is where using research meets with the real-world issues of *values* and *desirability*: you do not necessarily need to find the most effective outcomes, typically measured by improvements in examination results; rather, you should seek to pursue what is most effective from a range of outcomes that are desirable to you. Once you have established your values and the best way to pursue them, you can then seek to pursue change from a standpoint that is both values-based and research-informed.

KNOWING WHY AN EVIDENCE-INFORMED CHANGE IS GOING TO WORK AND UNDERSTANDING WHETHER IT HAS MADE A DIFFERENCE

Sarah Seleznyov's chapter (along with her chart differentiating teachers according to their quality of implementation of new practices and levels of use of these practices) also invokes the need to consider to theories of action (ToAs) (Argyris and Schön, 1978). ToAs help to explain how specific educational interventions or practices are constructed and why the innovators of those programmes believe they will work (Earl and Timperley 2015). More specifically, theories of action are perhaps best thought of as the journey guide for impact: they provide strategies – or route maps – that steer educators towards their intended long-term outcomes. Theories of action can also be seen as articulating the difference an innovation is designed to make for a given group or set of stakeholders. Correspondingly, to help educators reach this long-term vision, ToAs provide the steps that need to occur along the way. One suggested representation of a ToA comes from Brown (2019). Other examples occur in literature which synthesizes seminal impact measurement (e.g. Earl and Timperley, 2015; Earley and Porritt, 2013; Guskey, 2000; Wenger et al., 2011). Brown (2019) suggests that interventions can be conceived as being informed by and affecting change across a number of 'domains'. These domains are identified as:

- The **context** in which the relevant organization (e.g. a school or setting) is situated
- The **problem or driver** for the intervention or innovation
- Detail on **the intervention** and how it was intended to result in change
- **Activities and interactions** related to the introduction and roll-out of the intervention
- The **learning** that results from stakeholders engaging in these activities or from these interactions
- **Changes in stakeholders' behaviour** (e.g. teachers' or parents' behaviour), and the extent to which something is being used

- The **difference** stakeholder behavioural changes have made to a given target group's (e.g. children and young people's) outcomes

At the same time, Brown (2019) notes that using these dimensions to understand how an intervention works necessarily requires us to understand both the *why* and *how* of an intervention. Here the why refers to the logical operation of the intervention: the intended cause and effect that should result in a desired outcome or form of impact. Fixsen (2017), in order to explain the why of an intervention (such as for professional learning communities), uses a simple heuristic – a sequence of IF/THEN statements which result in a strategy for action. An example of Fixsen's approach is set out in box 1 below:

IF there are professional learning communities, THEN there will a scheduled time for teachers to discuss their work and the work students produce; and IF teachers share their work and the results with each other, THEN they will be able to learn from each other's successes and draw upon the expertise of their colleagues around common challenges (and so on until we reach impact for students).

Box 1: An example of Fixsen's use of IF/THEN statements.

The how, meanwhile, should set out in some detail the ways in which the why will be actualised. For instance, using the example above: How will scheduled time be created so that all relevant stakeholders can attend? How will teachers share their work in order to allow effective practice not only to be heard, but also to be engaged with and acted on? And so on. In other words, the *how* should provide a detailed description of the activities, resources, interactions, supporting structures, processes, policies and routines used to implement research-informed innovation to ensure that it has the desired effect. In particular the *how* includes the approaches that were or will be used to foster desired stakeholder learning, to encourage behaviour change amongst stakeholders and to support improvements in children's and young people's outcomes. With regards to research-informed practice, ToAs can and, we believe, should be used by teachers to generate understanding as to both why such practices were intended to work and how they should be operationalised in order to lead to positive change. The result is a project map to ensure the implementation of such practices is going to plan as well as a way of thinking about how to measure the impact of our changes.

IMPORTANCE OF PARTNERSHIPS AND COLLABORATIONS TO BETTER LINK THE WORLDS OF PRACTICE AND RESEARCH

One unfortunate side effect of Michael Gove's tenure as Secretary of State for Education was the characterisation of the education 'establishment' as The Blob (Gove, 2013) – something unhelpful and nebulous and that got in the way of school improvement. As a result, the view of many in relation to the value of effective partnerships between research and practice, universities and schools diminished. And yet in our view some of the most promising and successful instances of research-informed practice result when schools and universities work together. This view is shared in chapters by Andrew Morris, Jonathan Haslam, Vivienne Baumfield, and Karen Wespieser amongst others. The importance of partnership also emerges when we consider the backgrounds of many contributors who have either, as teachers, attained postgraduate qualifications (such as Claire Harley or Hanna Miller), or who have moved from academia to schools (e.g. Marcella McCarthy), or even vice versa (e.g. Dom Wyse, Stephen Gorard, and Vivienne Baumfield). Much access to research would of course not be possible without the likes of academic Steve Higgins, who has worked assiduously with the Education Endowment Foundation to author the *Teaching and Learning Toolkit*: a freely accessible resource that makes evidence easier to engage with. What's more, having pioneered partnership-centred concepts such as research learning communities (Brown) and the research-engaged school (Handscomb), we are in agreement, as Vivienne Baumfield argues, that the most effective way of engaging with research is one that helps marry this formal knowledge to what we know practically as teachers. Nonetheless, given the effort that is likely to be required if schools are to fully and effectively embed research use, it seems clear that teachers cannot go it alone here (Haslam).

SUMMARY

To summarise, then, from reading through the excellent work of our contributors we believe that to make research use a reality it needs to be made part of 'how things are done around here', it needs to be backed with resource, and knowledge relating to research and research-informed practice needs to be supported to flow around the school so that it can be accessed and engaged with. Schools also need to look beyond their gates and reach out to their local university school of education, who will likely be more than happy to work to support this process. But none of this should occur without the understanding that research use cannot be undertaken in absence of values and ethics. First and foremost, therefore, is having a clear vision for what we want for our children. Only then should we turn to research to help us achieve this.

REFERENCES

Argyris, C. and Schön, D. (1978) *Organizational learning: a theory of action perspective*. Reading, MA: Addison-Wesley.

Brown, C. (2019) 'Using theories of action approach to measure impact in an intelligent way: a case study from Ontario Canada', *Journal of Educational Change* [early online access].

Brown, C. and Flood, J. (2019) *Formalise, prioritise and mobilise: how school leaders secure the benefits of professional learning networks*. London: Emerald.

Earl, L. and H. Timperley (2015) *Evaluative thinking for successful educational innovation*. OECD Education Working Papers, No. 122. Paris: OECD Publishing.

Earley, P. and Porritt, V. (2013) 'Evaluating the impact of professional development: the need for a student-focused approach', *Professional Development in Education* 40 (1) pp. 112–129.

Fixsen, D. (2017) 'Implementation of educational interventions at the intersection of individual, organization, and institution', *Research on intervention and implementation in education – current state, challenges, and perspectives: Empirical Educational Research Conference*, Leibniz Association, Berlin, 22 May.

Gove, M (2013) 'I refuse to surrender to the Marxist teachers hell-bent on destroying our schools: Education Secretary berates "the new enemies of promise" for opposing his plans', *Daily Mail*, 23 March. Retrieved from: https://dailym.ai/2urH6LF [Accessed 10 December 2019].

Guskey, T. (2000) *Evaluating professional development.* Thousand Oaks, CA: Corwin Press.

Wenger, E., Trayner, B. and de Laat, M. (2011) *Promoting and assessing value creation in communities and networks: a conceptual framework.* Heerlen: Ruud de Moor Centrum, Open Universiteit.